My Friend,
The Bible

*Every problem we face can take us
one step away from God, or one
step closer . . .*

My Friend,
The Bible

JOHN SHERRILL

Published by

Lincoln, Virginia 22078
Distributed by Word Books • Waco, Texas 76703

Scripture quotations identified KJV are from the King James Version of the Bible.

Scripture quotations identified RSV are from The Revised Standard Version of the Bible, copyrighted 1946, 1952, © 1971 and 1973.

The Scripture quotation identified NAS is from the New American Standard Bible, Copyright © The Lockman Foundation 1960, 1962, 1963, 1968, 1971, 1972, 1973 and 1975.

The verse "A Word is Dead" on page 63 is taken from *Poems by Emily Dickenson*, edited by Thomas H. Johnson, and used by permission of Little, Brown and Company.

Library of Congress Cataloging in Publication Data

Sherrill, John L
    My friend, the Bible.

1. Bible—Use. 2. Sherrill, John L. 3. Christian biography—United States. I. Title.
BS538.3.S48   248'.2 [B]   78–15895

ISBN 0–912376–37–6

To
My Mother

Contents

Foreword 9
1. The Old Man's Promise 11
2. False Starts 19
3. The Trap of Inherited Emotions 26
4. Facing Problems in God's Company 35
5. Two Kinds of Power 48
6. Memorizing 57
7. The Partnership of Power 61
8. Counterfeit Suggestions for Power 65
9. Getting Specific—Even Though I'd Rather Not 72
10. Red Herring No. 1: Physical Problems 78
11. Red Herring No. 2: Problems in Our Work 90
12. Red Herring No. 3: The Spiritual Attack 104
13. The Unfolding Master Plan 112
14. Surprises and Adventure 121
15. When Problems Have No Answer . . . 133
16. The Best of All for Last 144
P.S. Full Circle 152
Appendix One: My Arsenal 155
Appendix Two: Bible Reading Programs 167

Foreword

MY FRIEND, THE BIBLE is a very personal account of the struggles of one man to find God's help with his everyday problems. John Sherrill has discovered that for him this help comes most dependably through the Bible.

But this discovery was neither easy nor automatic. John is a sensitive intelligent person who was trained to distrust "magic" approaches to life and faith. He had been a Christian for years but still felt daunted and even a little uncomfortable with the Bible. Scripture somehow always belonged to other people—his parents, the preacher, teachers, or those special saints we all know who seem to live in the Bible.

So when John was facing a problem and a friend challenged him to "stay close to the Word," he really didn't know how to begin. *My Friend, The Bible* is a roadmap of his journey, showing how he started, pointing detours and roadblocks, charting the practical techniques he has uncovered for letting the Bible help him meet everyday needs.

At this point John shares with us a dawning intimate experience—known by deeply committed Christians since the beginning—of "hearing" God "speak to him" particularly and specifically through the pages of the Bible. At first the rationally trained mind rebels. How can God speak to us across centuries and even contexts to shed light on our own problems and needs. And yet, when we are committed to the living Christ, our minds are open to the truth about ourselves and God's will; then the reflection of the Spirit's light off the words in the Bible often brings to our consciousness direction and strength-giving truths for living. Many Christians have experienced this over the centuries—even some who are much too sophisticated to admit it. But the strange alchemy of faith is such that one can sense God speaking to John (and to us) from depth to depth—from beneath the words and incidents in the Biblical drama to the deepest and even unconscious needs in our daily lives.

After he found the Bible to be a helpful companion in day-to-day issues John began to ask himself if it would be possible to find help with longer-standing, stubborn, darker problems in his life. In his book he boldly takes us with him into these frightening hidden arenas. John's problems were in the areas of bad personal relationships, physical appetites that were out of control, fears, sexual fantasies. These were John's individual battlefields, but as I read I found myself substituting my own particulars. And in doing so I began to see, as I had not, a way the Bible offers me, and anyone who will come to it as John did, a pathway to new depths of freedom and faith.

A word about John Sherrill himself. As editors at *Guideposts* magazine, John and his wife Tib (with their three children) have traveled a lot. In *My Friend, The Bible* we go with them to Africa, to South America, to Europe, all over the United States. This makes for colorful reading. But more important, John's work at *Guideposts* has made him a person trained to look for and anxious to share the ways in which faith can be applied to down-to-earth situations.

This book then is really the distillation of more than twenty years of experience and observation. But it is also a meeting with a very human, growing and seeking person who still has problems, but who has discovered a way to locate and deal with them through the Scriptures. Since many of us also still have difficulties being God's persons, we meet ourselves in *My Friend, the Bible*. And best of all we meet God in the very center of our problems, and of our temptations.

KEITH MILLER
Waco, Texas

1.

The Old Man's Promise

I FELT VAGUELY uneasy that Sunday morning several years ago as I looked around the bare, echoing room where my hostess was arranging child-sized chairs in a semicircle around her desk. I was visiting friends in a west Texas town. My hostess had asked me to attend the Bible class which she was teaching, and even before the class began I suspected that these men and women were going to know a *lot* more about Scripture than I did.

For as we had come into church a few moments earlier it seemed that every single person was carrying a Bible. It's just a cultural phenomenon, I said to myself. Back home in New York, in our own Episcopal church, if you brought a Bible with you on Sunday it meant you'd been asked to read the Epistle during the communion service. But this was not an Episcopal church in New York, this was a Baptist church in west Texas. And there were Bibles everywhere.

The classroom began to fill up. It was an old man who finally noticed that I was not carrying a Bible. I remember that he had a freshly scrubbed and sunbaked

11

face, and that he carried *two* Bibles. He put them down on a miniature chair, took his coat off, hung it carefully on a wall peg, and sat down. Then he spoke to me.

"Here, young fellow," he said, handing me one of his Bibles. I was gratified that someone could still call me *young*, since I was well past forty, at the time of that Texas visit, and what was left of my hair was already beginning to gray.

The old man couldn't let me have his *real* Bible, the large, black, leather-bound and dog-eared one. But he did hand me *The Living Bible* and I felt grateful. Not only for the loan, but because he had given me this particular version: I was one of those people who, in spite of the fact that I had been a Christian for several years, had read the Bible through eagerly shortly after my conversion, and had been an editor on an inter-faith magazine for years, still did not feel really comfortable with the Scripture. I couldn't seem to get a handle on the book. *The Living Bible*, though, in its green binding, seemed enough like any other book to put me at ease.

My hostess was handing out mimeographed sheets. When mine reached me I noticed with a shudder that it contained a list of Bible references. As surely as I sat in that kindergarten chair we would shortly be going around the circle, looking up passages and reading them aloud.

My eyes scanned the list. I wouldn't have trouble with Genesis, Exodus, Leviticus, Psalms, the Gospels, some of the Letters. But there were those other names on the list, the ones I could never find. Did Habakkuk come before or after Haggai? And for that matter, where was Haggai?

And then, sure enough, my hostess began at the far right. "Charles, would you please read our Philemon?"

Charles flipped to Philemon.

Quickly, I counted the number of chairs between me and Mr. Philemon, and found that I was Second Samuel. Not bad. I riffled the pages of *The Living Bible* and found Second Samuel.

By now it was the next person's turn: she had an easy reference in Acts.

But to my horror my hostess asked Mrs. Acts to read another passage too, which threw my count off. I was no longer Second Samuel. If my count were not thrown off again, I would be Titus. But if one other person should read two passages, I would be—Habakkuk!

I was hoping against hope that the Lord was not in a playful mood when an out occured to me. Maybe this Bible had an index!

While everyone was paying attention to Mr. Lamentations, I turned to the front of my *Living Bible* and sure enough, there was an index. Surreptitiously I held the book open to that page and waited. Mr. Lamentations finished. Mrs. Ezekiel read a short passage and then, as I had feared, another. I was next—I was Habakkuk! Even as my hostess was saying, "John, would you read the next passage?" my eyes were scanning the index. Sure enough, there it was. Page 715. With the smugness of a schoolboy who has been asked the one question he knows how to answer, I turned *right* to Habukkuk and started reading.

Just as I finished, a merciful bell rang and the class was over.

And then the first of two fragile events occurred, events which were separated by a few weeks of time but which were prophetic for me in the sense that in them I heard God speaking.

The first of these two statements came from the lips of the old man who had lent me his Bible. When it came time for me to give the Bible back to him, he asked the usual polite question.

"You here for long, fellow?" But then, without transition, the old man with the shining chin added the words which I know now came straight from God. He stroked his Bible and said,

"This is where you find the answers to your problems." That was all. The old man turned away.

But that afternoon as I was packing for the trip home I came across my own Bible. I took it out of my briefcase and in my mind compared its crisp pages with the much-fingered Bible the old man had brought with him. Why wasn't I using my Bible the way these people were? *This is where you find the answers to your problems* the old man had said. Was I missing something vital? Had these people discovered in their Bibles a quality I never dreamed of? In spite of that first eager reading after my conversion, the Bible remained for me a formidable book, the province of scholars and preachers and grandmothers, a book about God and about people who lived thousands of years ago. It just didn't occur to me that this was also a book about *me*.

It wasn't until another day, weeks later, that God spoke to me again about my relationship to the Bible.

And as so often happens, He spoke through the casual remark of a friend.

Back in 1959 I had had a second bout with cancer. Out of that fear-filled experience had come a direct, personal encounter with Jesus in a hospital room in New York. With it came a healing, and later a stunning, second personal encounter with the Holy Spirit, all of which I've described in a book titled *They Speak With Other Tongues*.

And that's where the trouble began. Because a book

that is even partially autobiographical always captures its author at a point in time. A person frozen on the pages of a book is different from the person who goes on living, changing, sometimes growing, sometimes regressing. People who met me in the pages of *They Speak With Other Tongues*, were not meeting the me of 1966 or 1971. Those first days after my conversion had been utterly joyful and strangely problem-free. But as time passed I began to recognize the shadow of old habit patterns. The sequence had a familiar ring because I had lived through it in my marriage to Tib. During the first blush of our love affair, our joy in finding each other was so great that we just didn't have time for problems. But the honeymoon wasn't the marriage. Nor was the ecstatic honeymoon experience of conversion what life with Jesus was all about. Bit by bit the Lord began to bring me down to earth, where real growth in Him must take place.

Oh, I didn't understand at the time that Jesus was involved in this reemergence of problems. Quite the contrary. Jealousy, anger, over-indulgence, sex-fantasies, fear —if I were the sort of person who had these problems, where was the victory Jesus had won for me! I tried my best to push down these ugly aspects of myself. When they wouldn't stay there, I felt more and more guilty.

And it was in the middle of this drift into guilty living that I found myself in west Texas, hearing an old man say that the Bible held the answer to our problems.

Just a few weeks later, because I am spiritually deaf and need to be shouted at, the Lord spoke to me a second time about the Bible.

Guideposts magazine, where Tib and I worked, was holding a writer's workshop in Holland. Between classes Tib and I sampled Dutch life. Ignoring the care she usually puts into her trim figure, Tib joined me in Holland's famous chocolate and pastry. Then, in reaction, we switched to raw herring and bicycled for miles along the canals. The little hotel where we were staying was all tile and thatched roof. Our room was on the third floor which you achieved by way of a series of ladders— the Dutch called them stairs.

Late one night after Tib had gone to bed I sat up talking with an old friend who was also one of the workshop teachers, Jamie Buckingham.

"I've been meaning to ask you, John," Jamie said, leaning back in his chair and crossing his hands behind his head, "how is your spiritual health?"

"Spiritual health?"

"Yes. You were talking at the workshop today about building scenes. Let's do just that. Here you are in Holland where you and Tib wrote *God's Smuggler*. Let's imagine that Brother Andrew has just driven up to this hotel from another of his Bible smuggling trips behind the Curtain. He hops out of his van and throws his arms around you, Dutch style, and starts to tell you about a narrow escape he had at a border search. He's having a praise service tonight to thank God for his safe return and he wants you to come. Now here comes the tension you're always telling writers to look for. Because on this same evening you *also* have a chance to spend time with some old drinking buddies. Which would you prefer?"

Silence.

"Maybe that's unfair. I know you don't care much for meetings. Let's try another scene. You're at home now. It's Sunday, and church time rolls around. Would you rather get your tomato plants out? Or, you and Tib have to make a decision. Is your first impulse to talk the issues through, or pray them through? In other words, what's your spiritual condition?"

And I had to admit the truth. Jamie was sensing something. My spiritual health was shaky and getting worse. I guess it showed. I never had been much of an actor.

So that night, into the small hours, Jamie and I talked about the ebb and flow of spiritual vitality. Jamie called this time the beginning of my Walk in the Spirit. The Leap, he said, launched us into the Christian dimension. The Walk was for life. It was on The Walk that each of us came to grips with his own nature.

And then, just as he was yawning and standing up to leave, Jamie asked that question.

He asked it casually. "How close are you staying to the word, John?"

"Do you mean the Bible? Well . . . I hear Scripture read each Sunday."

"That's a start. But do you read the Bible every day, by yourself?"

"No."

"Then start at once, John. Did you know that most vitamins have to be replenished daily? So does rest. So does muscle tone; your muscles start to deteriorate in three days without exercise.

"Your spirit's health follows the same law. If you don't stay close to the Bible, you'll get spiritually flabby within three days. Then if a problem crops up, you'll have no spiritual power to meet it with."

Jamie left. But I was thinking hard. Twice now I had heard the Lord speak about the Bible. Twice He linked His book to the problems I was facing.

I found that I could not forget that visit to Texas or that midnight scene in a small Dutch hotel. It was as if the Lord were saying: The time is here for a new kind of relationship between you and Me. Roll up your sleeves and get to work. He seemed to be urging me to begin by developing a new way of reading the Bible, not the

breathless, can't-lay-it-down experience I had known before, but a more disciplined, day-in, day-out approach.

All right. I would try it.

Being book-oriented I searched the library, went
through the volumes on our church's shelves, asked
around for good beginner's books about the Bible. There
were many such books, and interesting ones too. But I
could not find a single one that talked about the relationship between the Bible and the problems that had re-
asserted themselves in my life.

It looked as if I'd just have to plunge in, study the
Bible itself, and see what happened.

2.

False Starts

AS THE WEEKS passed Tib became worried about me.
I could tell, because she did *not* ask me to get all those
books off the dining room table. If I were going to draw
closer to the Bible, as Jamie advised, I was going to do
it better than anyone.

Spread all over the room where we ordinarily eat were
piles of books, loose-leaf binders, rows of freshly sharp-
ened pencils. There was not only a *Cruden's Concordance*, which listed thousands of Bible verses by their key
words, but also the much thicker *Strong's Concordance*.
There was the entire six-volume set of *Clarke's Commentary* which analyzed the Bible sentence by sentence in
quaint Victorian style. From *Guideposts* I borrowed first
one volume then another of the monumental *Interpreter's
Bible* and learned the difference between exegetical and
expository analysis.

"What is the difference, John?" asked Tib.

Patiently: "Exegesis is the science of interpretation.
Exposition is an application of the text."

"Oh."

The pile of books on the dining room table grew. There were Bible dictionaries, books that studied the Scriptures by theme, others that dissected the Bible by tracing its ancient manuscripts. Books that saw the Bible as literature or history, even two volumes that "proved the Bible false" by showing how many of the events had parallels in other nations' religious history.

About this time I was given an assignment by my editor at *Guideposts*. Seeing volumes of his *Interpreter's Bible* disappear every time I came into the office in New York (Tib and I work at our home in the suburbs), Len LeSourd said to me one morning,

"You seem to be unusually interested in the Bible these days, John. Come up with anything for a Spiritual Workshop?"

Spiritual Workshops were our teaching feature in the magazine. I leaned back and stared thoughtfully out the grimy window to the New York garment district below, "Well . . ." I tried not to sound *too* professional, "have you considered an analysis of which Pauline letters are really written by the Apostle?"

Len stared at me.

In the end he assigned me a theme on patience. So I went to work. Ten days later I had finished a document I was really pleased with. It was, in fact, quite probably the best piece of writing I had done for the magazine. The Workshop included quotes not only from the Bible but from giants like Tillich and Niebuhr and Barth. Tib and I always examine each other's material before turning it in. Usually Tib will have her comments back within the day. This time there was a strange silence. Finally I came right out and asked her, "Well?"

She didn't need to ask what the "Well?" went with. Her rich sense of humor broke forth in her laughing response. "Twenty-three footnotes, dear? For *Guide-posts?*"

I phoned Len to say that I was shelving the article for a month.

There seemed to be a peculiar truth about my Biblical research though. I had to put it to use, one way or another. At the next meeting of the prayer group Tib and I go to on Wednesday nights, I found myself, with a modest clearing of the throat, offering to "do a little teaching." Of course there wasn't much anyone could say, so I launched into a discussion of the Spirit's gift of patience, as it is found in the Bible. Half way through my presentation one of the women in the group interrupted. She had had a recent experience with patience which she wanted to share. I resisted the interruption. The Bible study was *my* province, and I resented her invasion of my territory. I kept steering the discussion back to the course I had charted, until one of the men laughed out loud:

"John, your ego is showing."

That was all, but I heard the message.

I can't speak for anyone else, but at least for myself I found a double danger in trying to draw closer to the Bible by starting my own private seminary. As important as scholarship is, I should leave that emphasis alone for now. It ran two risks. First, it tended to make me proud, as my friends swiftly pointed out to me. And second, the part of my makeup that needed building up right now was not so much my mind as my spirit. Scholarship put an emphasis on mind. Probably, one day, I would come back to Biblical analysis but it hardly seemed the place to start.

The next day I took Clarke and Cruden and Strong,

the Bible dictionaries and the rest of the weighty books off the dining room table. Some I returned to *Guideposts*. Others I put back on their shelves in my own library. Although I still use these books for reference and occasionally read Clarke just for fun, the effort to become a professor was over.

I didn't put away the paper and pencils however. I used them to rewrite the *Guideposts* Workshop on the theme of patience.

"*Now*," said Tib, an hour after I showed her the new version, "you've got something! Your piece is full of people instead of footnotes."

It was eleven o'clock on a summer's workday and I was still sitting in my favorite corner on the side porch, reading. The Bible. This time I wasn't studying about the Bible, I was studying the Bible, and although I sensed that this was a step in the right direction there was nevertheless something still out of kilter.

What a difference between the way I read the Bible now and the way I read it just after my conversion. The book was still fascinating but it had lost a lot of the newness and the reading, to be honest, had a forced quality about it. I'd get up at six and make coffee, thinking about people I knew, like David Wilkerson and Olivia Henry, who spent two, three, four hours a day "in the word." Well, if that was the way Bible reading was done, I'd do even better. I read and made notes, and smiled benignly on Tib when she came down at a reasonable hour to find the coffee already thick with age.

Of course, getting started with my work three hours late put a crimp on the day but I figured that was the price Bible readers often paid. Working at home has advantages for Tib and me. If I start at seven in the morning or at eleven, nothing but a little knot in my stomach knows the difference.

Or perhaps that's not exactly so. I remember my secretary waiting, evening after evening, while I tried to dash through correspondence I hadn't gotten to during the day. I remember a *Guideposts* re-write I didn't finish in time to make the issue because I'd been spending mornings with the Bible.

Bit by bit it began to occur to me that I was repeating the same error I had made with my effort at scholarship.

In both cases I was being competitive.

That is, I was comparing myself with others. I was trying to read the Bible *the way I saw other people reading the Bible*. I would be a better Bible scholar than anyone, or I would "stay in the word" longer than anyone. And if this created problems in my work, God would understand even if my boss didn't.

At last I saw clearly that when I spent too many hours reading the Bible I couldn't do my job right. And that was cheating.

Still I was determined not to drop my project just because I had made mistakes. One morning I decided that perhaps it would be a good idea to do something I should have done all along—pray.

"Lord," I said, "I'm trying to learn how to read the Bible. I'm not getting very far and I really need Your help."

It was while I was still praying that the insight came. Pride was the problem: it was pride that made me want to compete. "All right, Father. Please accept this as my Prayer of Yielded Pride. Help me to get my ego out of the way so that I can read the Bible as You direct me."

The early-morning sun flooded our porch and peace

settled over me such as I had not felt since I began this adventure. My own individual way of reading the Bible might or might not be different from other people's. The important element was to get competitiveness out of the way so that I could find the pattern that was right for me.

Ironically, the route out of competitiveness in Bible reading—for me—was to follow a pre-planned program used by thousands of other people.

The idea occurred to me one day when I was in the Washington Cathedral bookstore and saw a copy of the Episcopal Church Lectionary, published each year by Morehouse-Barlow.* I picked it up and immediately knew I had found my answer. For every day in the year, Bible references were given. Each morning and each evening there was a psalm, an Old Testament reading and a New Testament reading—and of reasonable length.

So I bought the lectionary and took it home. Right from the start I was glad I had made this choice. For I liked to think that each morning as I read a particular selection, our rector at St. Mark's was reading the same verse and so were thousands of other Christians across the country.

The lectionary, I soon discovered, had other advantages. It was designed to follow the unfolding Christian story through its main elements, always complete within one year. Each season had a special emphasis. Advent dealt with our need for repentance, Easter with victory, Trinity with service to others, and so on. So the lectionary gave a safe balance to reading: there was less chance of singling out pet passages and ignoring others.

Interesting how Tib, who had shown vast unenthusiasm for my efforts at scholarship and marathon reading, now

---

* See Appendix Two for other pre-selected reading programs.

seemed intrigued by what I was doing. Tib is a history buff; she especially valued the ancient roots of the lectionary system with its origins in Judaism. The Jews of Jesus' day too followed appointed reading in their synagogues. One day she said,

"What if I joined you? That way we'd be reading the same passages each day!"

And this was how I stumbled upon the second secret of sustained personal Bible reading. The first secret was to squelch the longer-than-thou syndrome by reading pre-set selections. The second was to make a pact with someone to read the same passages each day. My pact was with my wife but it could equally well have been with one of our children, or with someone in our prayer group or our church. Often Tib and I do not read the passages aloud, or even at the same time. But that's unimportant. What is important, we found, was the shared commitment.

I had barely got underway with my new approach to the Bible, however, before an unexpected difficulty began to emerge. I was carrying around inside me, I discovered, other people's feelings about the Bible. These feelings were still powerful. Although in many cases I had not seen the individuals since childhood . . .

3.

The Trap of Inherited Emotions

I HAD NO IDEA that I was carrying around a highly charged set of attitudes toward the Bible, picked up from other people. The greatest enemy of intellectual honesty is the opinion of people we value and respect. The people who fell into this category for me impressed their views on my mind with almost indelible force.

One morning when Tib and I sat down in our now-cleared dining room to read the Bible together, the first selection from the lectionary was Psalm 18. I began calmly enough.

> The Lord also thundered in the heavens,
>   and the Most High uttered his voice,
>   hailstones and coals of fire.
> And he sent out his arrows, and scattered them;
>   he flashed forth lightnings, and routed them.
>
> Psalm 18:13, 14 RSV

Suddenly my heart started to race, my stomach knotted. I put the Bible face up on the table beside me. "What in the world's the matter?" Tib asked.

"I don't know. It's something in this reading."

Tib picked up the Bible and glanced down the verses. "I don't understand. This psalm is telling about how Jehovah comes to our rescue in times of trouble. It's a poem full of images." She picked up the selection:

> He bowed the heavens, and came down;
> thick darkness was under his feet.
> He rode on a cherub, and flew;
> he came swiftly upon the wings of the wind.
>
> Psalm 18:9, 10 RSV

But all the while Tib was reading I kept having that same half-panicky reaction. Afterwards, our seventeen-year-old Liz came down for breakfast before catching the high school bus, and we did not get back to the subject.

Later that day however I forced myself to face what had happened. The fact was that those verses *had* left me upset. They brought back frightening half-forgotten memories. Memories of times when my father, usually the personification of calm, became agitated enough that my small-boy antenna picked up danger signals.

There was one man who came around often to the Presbyterian Theological Seminary in Louisville, Kentucky, where my father was a professor, whose name I never knew. Dad always spoke of the man simply as *him*. And he always spoke with emotion.

"You just can't reason with *him*, Helen." This, in a whispered aside to Mother.

"It's *him* again!" This, when Dad thought I was out of earshot. "Trying to divide the faculty."

Dad never discussed this squabble with me, but by the time I was ten I had picked up the main outlines. The emotion was attached to the question, How much of the Bible do you understand as literal and how much as figurative? *Him* and his school fought to hold the line against the school, represented by my father, which sought to place the Bible in an historical and literary framework. The Bible, according to *him,* was literally true in every detail and anyone who thought otherwise was going straight to hell. If the Bible said God rode a cherub, then that is precisely what happened and to read Scripture in any other way was to undermine the very foundations of Christian faith.

I wonder what Dad would say today if he were alive and knew that I, his own son, was far closer to the position of the literalists than I was to his own. I wonder how we would go about communicating on this subject because it's surprising how incapable Dad was of listening to anything this one man, *him,* had to say. That wasn't like Dad. People from all over the country came to our red brick house in the Highlands of Louisville to seek Dad's help with anguishing personal problems. They came because he was open hearted and knew how to listen. Yet with *him,* Dad never really tried.

The war spread. One winter day I happened to be with Dad in the living room as he was going through his mail.

"Not again!" he exploded, and then the words slipped out, "I'll bet *he's* behind this." I looked at the envelope Dad was holding. The letter wasn't from *him,* because *he* was an educated man and this envelope had been addressed in a pencilled scrawl. Dad ripped it open, glanced at it hurriedly, then threw both letter and envelope into the wastebasket.

I wanted to learn more.

"Who was that from?" I asked.

"A man who wants to fight with me," Dad said.

"No really, who is it from, Dad?" I fished the letter

out of the wastebasket and just had time to notice that
the pencilled return address was from a small town in
the mountains of Kentucky.

"It's not important," my father said, taking the letter
back and throwing it, this time, into the fire. "The man
is threatening me. Let's go see if lunch is ready."

I didn't enjoy that lunchtime, wondering if the man
would come and if he would shoot Mother and my sister
Mary and me as well.

So I learned about this controversy in a quite personal
way. Men of liberal thought were asking questions. How
did science mesh with the truth revealed in the Bible?
How did modern psychological insights fit the Biblical
viewpoint? Dad was one of the early pioneers in the
now widely accepted discipline of pastoral counseling.
And the truth he perceived did seem to bear fruit. Dad's
own caring insights brought wholeness to young pas-
tors. He could relate the story of Jesus' healing the
withered hand so inspiringly that men were, in fact, transformed.

As a boy I observed all this, and I was impressed.
Heroes and villains were clearly outlined. Heroes were
people who tried to be honest in their thinking, even
though it shattered taboos. Villains—at the time, it never
even occurred to me to think otherwise—were those
who held to the literal interpretation of the Bible.

In time I too came in for hostility. I remember once
in my early teens going with my father and mother to a
fashionable white-pillared home in a well-to-do section
of Louisville. It was a small gathering, half a dozen families, and it soon became clear that one particular guest, a
lanky Scotsman with heavy, bright red eyebrows, was
keeping a weather eye on me. I even wondered if this
man were *him,* and he may indeed have been, for half
way through the party he cornered me on the sunporch

and made me sit down. I remember how his red eyebrows bobbed up and down as he commanded me to pay
attention. He was going to straighten me out on the
Bible, this same Bible which he held in his hand. If my
eyes wandered, the Scotsman would reach over and
grasp my chin and twist my face around so that I was
forced to look at him. "Listen to me, John. It says right
here that the flood covered the whole earth. That means
all of it, every continent, every mountain top."

People who believed the Bible, it seemed, weren't even
kind. People who respected the Bible but didn't *believe*
much of it were considerate. Maybe they didn't find much
mystic support from Scripture but they believed man
should be strong in the face of his troubles.

Dad was. A few years after my encounter with the
Scot of the flaming eyebrows, while I was in basic training in the Army, Dad went almost totally blind. All he
had left was a little peripheral vision that let him walk
around his classroom or apartment. He went right on
with his teaching and writing schedule, reading more,
(through braille and Talking Books,) than I did.

After he lost his eyesight Dad was called to Union
Theological Seminary in New York. The only dishonesty
I ever caught him at was an odd one. Dad thought blind-
ness was disconcerting to people, distracting them from
what he was saying. So he carried notes to his lectern in
class or turned pages of the Bible in the pulpit at the
Union chapel, pretending to read but in fact reciting by
heart passages locked in his phenomenal memory. Once
years later I met a man who had been a student under
Dad at Union. He heatedly refused to believe that my
father had been unable to see.

So, as I say, I had a real hero to look up to and admire
in Dad, and some pretty unpleasant people in *him* and

his ilk. And my considered view of the matter received still further support.

I'll never forget as a new reporter for *Guideposts*, being sent by the magazine to interview a trapeze artist who was also an evangelist. I caught up with the aerialist in a little church in Vermont where he was holding services.

It happened, the week before the revival, that there had been a collision outside of town between a gasoline truck and a private automobile. In the fire that followed the car's two passengers were burned to death. The night I was there, with a kind of sick glee the trapeze artist described the deaths in crackling detail, then compared that fearful event to the unquenchable fires of hell that we would all most certainly experience if we did not come forward then and there in answer to his altar call.

So I was pretty well conditioned to react negatively to the subject of Biblical literalness.

And I don't think I am alone in having these visceral emotions. Most of us, approaching the Bible, bring to it a set of preconceived notions and subconscious assumptions which we have inherited from our past. Some of us grew up feeling that the Bible is not important one way or another; it is simply another ancient book. Others unconsciously disparage it, putting it down as the province of ignorant people and associating it with an Elmer Gantry mentality. Still others may bring to the Bible an almost idolatrous attitude, like a friend of ours who will never place another book, or even a pencil, on top of it, a carryover from the days when few people could read, and the Bible was processed through the church as an object of worship.

The point is that just about everyone carries around attitudes toward the Bible which predate his actual ex-

perience with it. In my own case, I had a lot of ground-
work to do before I could examine the question of Biblical
literalness. I had to identify the childhood emotions I
was bringing to the subject and then, to the best of my
ability, suspend those reactions and start afresh, letting
the Bible speak to *me*.

And in the meanwhile some very different experiences
had to be woven into my understanding of the world
around me.

The first experience was the physical healing to which
I referred at the opening of this story. How fresh the
scene remains for me. There I was, kneeling with Tib
before the little altar in our hometown church in Mt.
Kisco, New York, shortly after I'd been told my cancer
had returned. There was our parish priest, Marc Hall,
standing behind us. Now he was laying his huge hands
on my head in the ancient healing rite of the church. I
was numbed, afraid. But suddenly something happened
which broke through this dullness. Marc's hands had
barely touched my head when power surged through
him, entered my body, burning. The heat localized at the
very place where the head-and-neck specialist at New
York's Memorial Hospital had identified the return of
those damning lumps. We left the church, and checked
into the famous cancer hospital. The surgeon operated,
just hours after the prayer for healing. He found nothing
but dried up nodules.

The second event took place shortly after the first.
Now it is late at night. I am in my room at Memorial
Hospital just after coming down from Recovery. I am
in intense pain, but two other men in the room with me
seem to be in still worse condition; one is coughing so
desperately that I worry for his life; the other, a young-
ster, is moaning in agony. Quietly, softly into that dark
hospital room comes a light which at first I assume is a

light carried by a nurse, so real, so illuminating is it. But the light grows in intensity. In warmth. In . . . personality. I know Who it is. In the company of that infinite caring the first thing that occurs to me is to ask Jesus to touch my two roommates. Jesus responds. The coughing stills. The moans stop.

The third event took place in an ordinary hotel room in Atlantic City, New Jersey. A few Christians had come here to pray with me for the Baptism in the Holy Spirit. At first I was self-conscious and resisting. But then . . . into my mind came the memory of my encounter with light. That night in the hospital, I had been able to concentrate on Jesus only. And so it was now too. Suddenly, from deep within begins a joyous, powerful communication so direct and intimate that I cannot contain it. I hear my own voice speaking a language I never learned.

These three experiences represented something new. My cancer was healed, not figuratively but literally. The light I saw in the hospital room was able to reach out and touch suffering men. Speaking in tongues was an audible phenomenon, not a figurative way of stating that God can enable man to communicate.

As I cautiously came to grips with the literalness of these events I saw that I had some serious thinking to do.

Maybe Dad was wrong.

Maybe, for instance, the man in the synagogue that Sabbath had a physically shriveled up hand, just as the Bible said. It seemed more and more likely that flesh and bone had changed in front of a disbelieving congregation and that from then on the man had a workable hand. From what I had seen in my own life I was ready to believe that this was a literal, precise description of what Jesus did one day.

So my understanding was making a huge arc. I started

out with an emotional heritage which told me that most of the Bible was allegory. I still did not see *everything* in the Bible as factual description. Some passages are poetic, some are meant to be understood as figure. A good example is in Jesus' statement, "Except a man be born again, he cannot see the kingdom of God." Nicodemus tried to take this literally, asking, "How can a man be born when he is old? Can he enter the second time into his mother's womb, and be born?" But Jesus corrected him with some amusement, "Art thou a master of Israel, and knowest not these things?" He then went on to explain the metaphor (John 3:3, 4, 10 ff. KJV).

With these clear exceptions I was beginning to see larger and larger portions of the Bible as descriptions of literal events.

But truth dwelt in these accounts at a still deeper level. As I was grasping the huge fact of literalness, I was still only part way into the awesome reality of this Book.

For the truth in the Bible was also contemporary. It had happened then; it was also happening now. Even literalness was not so important as tense.

And even *this* was not the end of the adventure. I had to see these present-tense events as happening *to me*. I *am* a kind of Abram, setting out from my own familiar homeland, not knowing what lies ahead. I *am* one of the believers gathered in the Upper Room as we are all filled with the Holy Spirit. I *am* a man who has been told he will soon die, a man whom Jesus heals.

What a turnabout. I do wish Dad were alive so we could talk about these things. What would he say if one night we sat quietly by the fire and I finally confided to him how I've come to feel. Could I tell this man how much I love him . . . but think he was wrong?

4.

Facing Problems
In God's Company

TEN MINUTES AGO Tib and I had landed at LaGuardia Airport where we were met by our son Donn, who had just finished college. Donn took our bags and with his athletic skills showing, dodged New Yorker-style through traffic to the parking lot.

All the while he was talking about how mixed-breed dogs were superior to full-blooded animals.

"For example," Donn said, as he put our suitcases in the trunk, "there's the blend of Husky and German Shepherd. Friend of mine says this is the ideal mix."

On the way to the exit ramp: "A man ought to have a dog."

At the toll gate on the Whitestone Bridge: "A good watchdog is important these days."

A little later at a self-service station, while Donn was filling the tank, Tib took off her glasses and let out a sigh. "Like it or not there's a puppy sitting in our basement this minute."

I stared at her. As our three children one by one left home, the house had taken on a welcome calm. Tib and

I could go to bed early, leave on interview trips with no more forethought than turning the lock on the front door. Suppose Tib were right and Donn did have a dog in our basement. My mind leaped ahead to the interference this would bring. The animal would probably bark all night. I once knew a Husky who bit little children. I'd also known a Shepherd who went for the throat first and growled later. Besides, Donn hadn't talked this over with us. He waited until we were away on a trip . . .

Donn was replacing the hose. "Do you know for sure?" I whispered quickly to Tib. "That he has a dog, I mean."

"I know Donn for sure. All this propaganda's leading somewhere."

I spent the next twenty miles talking—as if theoretically —about the impossibility of having a dog, especially a young, noisy one, with our offices at home, and our trips so frequent. Donn was silent.

We pulled into our driveway. "Let's go through the basement," Donn said heavily.

And there, of course, was the dog.

Donn had rigged up a pen next to my basement office. The pup's stomach was distended, one ear flopped forward, one back, his tail whirled. He was visibly untrained.

He didn't look much like a cross between German Shepherd and Husky, either. I asked Donn about that.

"I told them at the pound . . ." Donn picked up his dog, "what I wanted. Just by *coincidence* the man happened to have my dog." Tib raised her eyes skyward.

For the rest of the day no one brought up the subject of dogs. But the battle was on nevertheless. I told Donn we were angry because he had gotten the dog behind our backs. Donn was leaving home in a couple of months to do graduate work in International Business Management but until then, he said, this was still his home and didn't he have a right to have a dog if he wanted one!

So the battle went on. But wouldn't this be a perfect opportunity to probe further the idea of the old man in Texas, that in the Bible we can find answers to our problems? Could it be that the Bible spoke to homely everyday problems such as I was facing with this odd threat to my peace? I'd find out.

Next morning, waked early by Donn's dog, I got up, made coffee and went down to my office intending to read the daily lectionary there. But the basement reeked. Annoyance pricked me again. I was all the more aggravated because I had to admit the little animal was friendly! I started to pick up his fouled newspaper but decided against it. No, this was Donn's dog and the mess went with him, too.

Back upstairs, I went into the living room, sat down in my favorite corner of the sofa and opened my Bible to the psalm appointed for that morning. To be honest, I wasn't expecting much to happen. It was the 47th Psalm:

Clap your hands, all peoples!
Shout to God with loud songs of
    joy!
For the Lord, the Most High, is
    terrible,
    a great king over all the earth.
He subdued peoples under us,
    and nations under our feet.
He chose our heritage for us,
    the pride of Jacob whom he loves.

I was right. Nothing to do with that dog!

God has gone up with a shout,
    the Lord with the sound of a
    trumpet.
Sing praises to God, sing praises!
    Sing praises to our King, sing
    praises!

For God is the king of all the earth;
sing praises with a psalm!

Psalm 47:1–7 RSV

I put the Bible down abruptly! I couldn't go on. There was something in this second stanza that caught my attention for reasons which I could not understand. That stanza seemed important somehow, as if it were speaking just to this situation. Sing praises . . .

I sat up straighter. Upstairs I heard someone stirring. Sing praises.

Why did this phrase seem to have a peculiar sticking quality? I was especially puzzled because the very word "praise" had been a problem to me. I knew too many people who abused it, using it on every occasion, often with a peculiar sing-song lilt. "Well pa-raise God!" They used it as a synonym for "thanks." "Praise You, Lord! Thank You, Lord, for letting my son catch pneumonia!" When you are *thankful* to someone for something you imply that he is responsible. And I couldn't understand how God could cause a child to catch pneumonia, nor for that matter could I believe that He had put a yelping little creature in my basement.

But the phrase wouldn't let me go. I remembered my friend Bill Henley, a member of our prayer group, once pointing out that praise is *trust*. That did change the overtone of the word. It shifted the time emphasis from the past to the future. Praise was not so much thanking God for what has happened, as trusting Him for what is going to happen. The element of joy is based on what is to come. "Praise You, Lord. I trust Your love, even though my son has pneumonia."

Was that why I had been stopped? "Are You saying Lord, that You want me to trust You today, even in this annoying situation? I worry about my precious peace instead of trusting You. I'm not counting on You to grant me enough quiet for my work. This is why I got so upset with Donn."

Even as I spoke my heart lifted. I went back to the psalm and read again, rapidly, for I heard footsteps on the stairs. "Sing praises to God . . ." Trust Him for what's going to happen. "Lord" I said quickly, under my breath, as Donn came into the living room, "I do trust You with this dog. I believe that You can turn it into something wonderful . . ."

"Morning, Donn," I said aloud. "Sleep well? Your dog will be mighty glad to see you."

I don't want to lean too heavily on one little dog, but it is in these intimate adventures that a lot is revealed. Donn decided to call his dog Lobo, Spanish for *wolf*. That same day while I was practicing trust, Lobo began to show symptoms that were alarming. He was vomiting, and his stomach looked more than usually distended. Donn took his dog to the vet, who insisted on keeping him overnight. Donn returned deflated and reported the vet as saying, "That dog is no mixture of Shepherd and Husky. If I read the signs right, you'll have to change his name from Lobo to Lobito." Lobito means little, very little wolf.

I was making some progress toward appropriating a new attitude about Donn's dog. That night before putting out the light I turned to the evening readings, and as had occurred that morning, a passage seemed to call attention to itself. Again, the portion happened to be from a psalm. The writer recounted all the help God had given Israel, yet the people continually grumbled. They doubted that God could spread a table in the wilderness even though He had just supplied them with water.

Therefore, when the Lord heard, he
    was full of wrath;

a fire was kindled against Jacob,
his anger mounted against Israel;
because they had no faith in God,
and did not trust his saving power.

Psalm 78:21, 22 RSV

The message of this strangely highlighted section was extremely clear. I was behaving in the same way that the people of Israel had acted. I was grumbling. I was unhappy with the dog and with Donn because I "had no faith in God, and did not trust his saving power."

That same night I determined by simple willpower not to let this doubting go on. For twenty minutes by the clock I recalled times when God's power had come to help us. I thought of Donn's dog, sitting now in a dark cage at the vet's. I spoke aloud to Tib the first words to come into my mind.

"Do you suppose Lobo's all right?"

Tib looked at me amused. "That dog's getting through to you, isn't he?"

"Something is. That's for sure."

The next morning, early, Donn went down to get his dog. Lobo was all right, thank You, Lord. The vet thought the vomiting stemmed from a poor diet before Lobo came into our household.

Donn put his dog in the pen downstairs. Later that morning I came out of my office and saw Lobito in his usual position, standing on his hind feet, tail whirling.

I reached down and patted him.

Then I found myself picking him up.

Surreptitiously, I took him out to the back yard and let him chase me. Right at the height of the romp I happened to glance toward the dining room window.

There stood Tib and Donn. They were both laughing.

Words That Burn

A strange thing had happened twice in a row. It had been as if the Bible were mysteriously activated, so that a portion was charged with power intended just for my right-now situation.

Something similar to this had happened to the disciples themselves. Discouraged, defeated, lost, they met the resurrected Jesus on the road to Emmaus. He seemed at first to be just another traveler. But then His words began to take a peculiar turn. "Did not our hearts burn within us while he talked to us on the road, while he opened to us the scriptures?" the disciples later asked (Luke 24:32 rsv). It was the same phenomenon I had experienced reading the Bible. My heart burned within me as specific words were illuminated.

Could it be that Jesus is still opening the Scriptures to us? Individually? Now? As we face specific problems?

The question was so vital that I began asking other Christians if they had noticed the same thing and almost without exception they had. People used different words to describe this mysterious activity. Some said words "stopped" them; others said the words made them pay attention or "leaped out of the page;" still others said that words were "spotlighted" or that "they seemed to speak aloud." But always the message was the same: the Bible had a way of talking individually to the reader through words that burned.

As if to encourage me in my discovery, the next week I found these words on the back of a calling card:

"I am sorry for the men who do not read the Bible every day. I wonder why they deprive themselves of the strength and of the pleasure. It is one of the most singular books in the world, for every time you open it, some old text that you have read a score of times suddenly beams with a new meaning. There is no other book that I know of, of which this is true: there is no other book that yields its meaning so personally, that seems to fit itself so intimately to the very spirit that is seeking its guidance." The words were Woodrow Wilson's.

It is hard to describe the excitement I felt. I had a new reason for reading the Bible. Every day I could bring some real-life situation to the Scriptures. It could be a problem, an intercession, a decision, my own need or someone else's. With this on my mind I would read until Jesus spoke to me through words that glowed.

And so I began a life-changing experiment. One day the beaming verse would speak words of encouragement, another day words of correction. They might bring specific instruction or simply an expression of His love. But the verses always had one thing in common. They were unbelievably on target. They always spoke as a person would speak who knew me thoroughly, who knew what I was facing, who grasped my situation, from the tiniest details to the overall picture, far more clearly in fact than I did myself.

One morning, for instance, I faced an emergency deadline. I had to do three days' worth of work for the magazine in just a few hours, a situation that called for more energy and boldness than I possessed. That day Mark 4:40 spoke directly to me. "And he said unto them, Why are ye so fearful? how is it that ye have no faith?" Every time during that day when my enervating fears rose up, this verse had the power to encourage.

On another day I had just watched a spectacular sunset, only to open the Bible to the appointed readings, "The heavens are telling the glory of God; and the firmament proclaims his handiwork" (Psalm 19:1 RSV). Tib began to have the experience too. On the first night of a visit to the whaling center of Nantucket she read,

> Yonder is the sea, great and wide,
>   which teems with things
>   innumerable,
>   living things both small and great.
> There go the ships,
>   and Leviathan which thou didst
>   form to sport in it.
>
> Psalm 104:25, 26 RSV

Sometimes the stopping verse took on a correcting note. One day I was suffering an unusual kind of pain. We were in the middle of a seven-months-long drought in New York. Corn, which should have been "knee high in July," was barely six inches tall. Our lawn had browned out but watering was forbidden. The creek in our back yard was a trickle. Trees curled their leaves in protest.

Now, I have never understood why water, plenty of water, is so important to me. Tib loves the desert, but I do not. Lack of water causes me personal pain. I try to pull moisture out of the air. I yearn for it, suffer with the ground. It is a visceral experience, beyond logic.

One morning during my living room reading time I was again feeling this pain when suddenly a set of words came into sharper-than-usual focus.

"Offer to God a sacrifice of thanksgiving . . ." (Psalm 50:14 RSV).

What did that mean? I tried to read on, but the verse pulled me back. I *could* give thanks, of course, right in this drought, as an act of will. But it would indeed be a kind of sacrifice, a costly and difficult thing to do in the midst of the arid reality I saw around me.

"I think I'm hearing You, though," I mused, there at my sofa-corner post in the living room. "I doubt You want me to give thanks for the drought itself, but I can live through my Sahara in an attitude of thanksgiving. I give You thanks for the water we do have. Thanks for the abundant crops we usually enjoy. Thanks for the fact that we have plenty of food." The rest of the day whenever dust eddies blew past the window I deliberately put myself into a mood of appreciation and thankfulness, even when a negative mood would have *seemed* appropriate.

It made all the difference. Not just for that day, but for the duration of the drought. I was able to live through the rest of the almost rainless summer in an attitude of joy by leaning on this verse from the Psalms.

So my experiment proceeded. I kept at my reading, confident that I would receive a special word from the Lord each day.

Then one morning, after I had been at my program for some weeks, a strange thing happened. No illuminated verse appeared. The next day was the same. Occasionally, over the following two weeks, I would be given a highlighted verse, but it lacked force and immediacy. Which perhaps explains why, when words at last did make themselves known to me in the familiar, blazing way, I felt a sense of great excitement.

"If I had cherished iniquity in my heart, the Lord would not have listened," said Psalm 66:18 (RSV).

"All right, Lord, there must be something between us. Would you tell me what it is?"

Almost immediately sprang to mind a still-smarting memory. Just a couple of weeks before (right at the time I began to have trouble hearing God in the Bible) I had been cheated out of two hundred dollars. Tib and I have long wanted to own a piece of land on which we might, some day, build a smaller, retirement house. I saw an ad in the *New York Times* for several acres of wild rocky land that sounded just exactly right and called the number. Soon I was traipsing over hills, talking about perc tests and imagining where a house could go.

"I'm trying to settle an estate," the owner told me. "That's why this price is so low. Are you interested?"

"Definitely. But I want my wife to see it."

"Sorry. Other people are . . ." He didn't finish his sentence because an idea occurred to him. "Why don't you just put down a binder? It doesn't have to be much. Two hundred will do. If you change your mind I'll give you your money back."

Which I did. Tib came with me the next day to see the property and we both agreed that it was just right. So I called up the owner and told him he had a deal.

"Well . . ." he said. "You see . . ."

And I knew there was a problem. The owner had decided not to sell after all. He was sorry. I was disappointed, but I didn't want to hold him to his binder, so the owner agreed to send me a check since he had already cashed my own. Three days passed. A week. No check. I called the owner and received an astonished, "You haven't got your money yet! I'll speak to my secretary. It'll be in the mail today." Nothing. That went on for another week with my phone calls becoming more and more frequent. I asked an attorney what I could do and he assured me that recovery would cost more than the two hundred.

So I quit calling, but my emotions were still fighting. In my mind I played and replayed conversations with this man if he ever did call back. Which he didn't.

"Do you know where he lives?" Tib asked when I brought up my dilemma at the supper table. "If he won't return your calls you could go over there."

Which we did, that same night. The owner's house was dark. A neighbor was walking a dog. "They've gone to Florida for the winter," he told us.

I started to back out of the man's driveway, defeated. "You can't just leave, honey," Tib said. "You haven't resolved a thing."

"There's nothing more I can do. Unless maybe we sit here and pray for the guy." I was half joking, but Tib treated the idea seriously. So, there in the owner's driveway, she and I said what was, for us, an unusual prayer. We released the owner from any judgment on our part. We couldn't see him face to face, but we asked the Lord to heal whatever hurt there was in his life that made him act in a way that must be costing him peace and joy too.

Tib turned on the domelight and looked at me closely. "Lord," she added, "You know how upset this has made John. If there is anything left in him of anger, hurt pride, feeling that he should stand up for his rights, we just ask You to take that over too. Do for John what he can't do for himself."

"Amen," I said.

And the results? We never did get our two hundred back. But that night the Scriptures opened to me again. ". . . fret not thyself because of him who prospereth in his way, because of the man who bringeth wicked devices to pass" (Psalm 37:7 KJV). I was accustomed to apropos readings but this one was astonishing. It was as if the Lord were saying, "It's good to have your ear again."

So that was the beginning of what was, for me, a new way to read the Bible. I found that illumination could shine on just a few words or on a whole section. The stopping verse could come immediately, or at the end of the reading, or even, indeed, outside the prescribed reading altogether. I learned to put down my Bible for a moment when I got to my verse. I would live with that word, mull it over, listen.

Sometimes the lectionary wasn't involved at all. One day I was in Houston on a story for *Guideposts*. The interview with the astronaut went badly and I knew that I had failed in my assignment. There was no point writing up my slim notes so I was left with a lot of time on my hands, disappointed, far away from home . . . a bad combination for me.

And to make matters worse I had forgotten to bring my Bible and lectionary. I opened the formica drawer in the formica table in the motel room and there, among the laundry lists and room service cards, was a Gideon Bible. I opened it, flipped idly through the pages, browsing in Isaiah. I began to read the 62nd chapter. Nothing. I read on, into the next chapter. Nothing.

But then there it was, complete and satisfying, an illuminated single phrase. At first it didn't seem apropos: "In all their affliction he was afflicted . . ." the passage said (Isaiah 63:9 KJV). But then I understood. The Lord Himself was sharing this disappointment and this boring evening with me. He knew all about the failure, too. He was hurting with me and could empathize.

I picked up the phone and called home to have a long, leisurely talk with Tib. All that evening and all the way back home without my story I felt excited. What a helpful passage! What a useful tool!

5.

Two Kinds of Power

TWO DAYS LATER I was thinking again about that experience in Houston. I opened my Bible to the passage I had found and read it over. "In all their affliction he was afflicted . . ." I expected a return of the excitement I had experienced there in my hotel room, when I had been so frustrated and lonesome and had been strongly supported by the Bible.

Instead, the verse seemed flat.

What was the matter? How could a verse be full of life one day, seemingly empty the next? I went through my Bible to see if this were also true of other passages which seemed so vital when I first read them. Time after time it was true. The Psalm passage that helped me praise God for Lobo—it seemed a bit ordinary now. The reading that lifted "my" sunset into still another realm of glory—when I read it over now, it seemed lackluster. It was almost as if the passages had been infused with unusual life for those special occasions.

Manna Verses

Maybe it was like that hibiscus. Tib's grandparents lived in Miami Beach. Every morning Papa went into his backyard to pick a red hibiscus blossom for Goggie's breakfast table. The first time I saw him do this I was surprised that he simply placed the fragile crepe-like bloom on the table.

"Shouldn't that flower be in water?" I whispered to Tib. Tib smiled at my northern innocence. "That wouldn't help," she explained. "There's nothing you can do to keep an hibiscus blossom. Whether you leave it on the table or put it in water, it can last for just one day."

And so had that verse I found in the hotel room in Houston. Were highlighted verses often *meant* to last only for a span of time? Perhaps for the space of a particular project, where pinpointed direction or support was especially needed? Perhaps, sometimes, for a week or just a day or even for a few hours. It would make sense. There is a here-then-gone quality about so many valuable things. A smile, a snowflake, a perfect family meal with everyone there. This is often God's way of giving us His favorite gifts too. I re-read Exodus 16, where Moses is explaining manna to Israel. It was the bread which the Lord had given the people to eat, Moses said. But it was a right-now gift:

> Morning by morning they gathered it, each as much as he could eat; but when the sun grew hot, it melted.
>
> Exodus 16:21 RSV

Manna was sufficient, perfect food for a span of time. But if it was kept past that time, then it spoiled (Exodus 16:20) or melted (Exodus 16:21). And so it was with many stopping-verses. Later, if I went back over the reading, the once brimming passage just didn't speak in the same way. I could still remember the warmth and security that had come to me, yesterday, when I had been held close by God, but it was just a memory; like a dream, it was almost impossible to recapture the sense of immediacy I had experienced the day before.

Apparently the Lord wanted me to come to Him each day for mystic fellowship to see me through that day's needs.

I must admit that I had a nag-and-pester worry. It started as a fleeting question, but grew in intensity. Maybe there was nothing truly supernatural in these Manna Verses, nothing unexplainable about what was happening. Perhaps it was just an accident. Could I have found help because I *wanted* to find it, nothing more?

Then, one morning, these words were singled out for me.

> For we have not a high priest who is unable to sympathize with our weaknesses, but one who in every respect has been tempted as we are, yet without sin.
>
> Hebrews 4:15 RSV

What was this verse saying to me! I actually tried to ignore the subtle brightness because it just wasn't germane to any problem I could think of; I was not aware of special temptations at the moment.

Then in that afternoon's mail came a royalty report. It was clear even at a glance that the publisher had made a mistake in our favor. A decimal place had got in the wrong column and we were being paid ten times the amount we were supposed to receive. Tib and I had unusual dental expenses that month and the larger check would have been welcome indeed.

But the temptation never had a chance. For there was the highlighted Manna Verse from that morning. I repeated it aloud, hearing it tell me that Jesus sympathized with my temptations, that He had been tested too, and yet He had not sinned. With Him as high priest interceding, it was a simple matter—a very simple matter really—to pick up the phone and get the error straightened out.

But wait a minute! As I put the phone back in its cradle I had a spinetingling realization. I had not brought this temptation to the Bible and then received a Manna Verse. It was the other way around. Something strictly supernatural had occurred. This Manna Verse was highlighted for me *before* the temptation took place. It couldn't have been me, looking for a helping hand and finding one. The word was given beforehand; then when it was needed, there it was ready to defend me.

But an even more unexplainable event occurred a few weeks later. On that morning, as I sat reading, a verse again "lit up" that didn't seem to have relevance to my life; perhaps this too was being highlighted for a problem-in-the-future.

"Blessed are they that do his commandments," the verse said, "that they may have right to the tree of life, and may enter in through the gates into the city" (Revelation 22:14 KJV).

I simply could not imagine how that passage would ever be important. I waited all through the afternoon, expectantly. Nothing came up that had any conceivable bearing on the quote.

Suppertime came and I was as puzzled as ever. Tib was out of town and I had a dinner date with a young bachelor who was planning to sell his grocery business and go into full-time work with runaway kids in New York City. My bachelor friend thought the Lord had told him to make the move, yet lately everything had come to a stop. No buyer appeared for his store, the work he had already begun with young people in the city seemed to stagnate. He couldn't tell why.

How can I describe the feeling of awe as I saw suddenly that the verse I had memorized that morning might fit not my situation but my friend's? "Blessed are they that do his commandments, that they . . . may enter into the city." Was he *not* entering his city because he was in some particular *not* doing the Lord's commandments? Yet how dare I bring that up!

We went on eating for ten minutes, with my verse humming in my mind, struggling, I suppose, to be expressed.

Finally I could take it no longer.

"Stan," I said, "are you by any chance disobeying God in some way?"

Stan began to stir his coffee so rapidly that it spilled out over the side of his cup.

I then explained why I was asking that question, quoting to him the verse that had been singled out of my morning-time reading.

Stan stirred his coffee, on and on. Finally, he took the spoon out, flicked off a last drop and leaned back.

"You *couldn't* have known," he said hoarsely.

Then he told me about an affair he was having with a married woman. It was a liaison, he said, that he now knew he would have to break if he ever wanted to enter his city and be effective with young people.

"It's not that I *didn't* know before," he said in a whisper, still awed, "it's that I didn't want to hear. But that verse of yours . . ." He laughed, not wanting to finish the sentence. And indeed he didn't need to go on. We both had witnessed the Lord in the act of stating how intimately He knows us, how individual is His caring.

Arsenal Verses

Tib and I were in Chicago for book interviews with Demos Shakarian, an Armenian dairyman who was a spearhead figure in the charismatic movement in the United States. Demos is a remarkable man in a great many ways, not the least of which is his energy. He thrives on long conventions and five-hour banquets, *then* wants to start our interviews.

And Demos was calling to ask if we could meet for some work just after midnight. We agreed, but I knew what would happen. Tib would give out around two but Demos would want to tell just one more story.

And that's what did happen.

There I was, sleepy and tired, yet anxious because I knew our schedule did not mesh easily with the Shakarians'. While Demos was pouring the last of the coffee from a silver hottle, I found myself wondering if there were any way I could use the Bible in this situation. Unfortunately Demos was now in the middle of the story of a remarkable bull-calf he once bought. It wouldn't do to just stop life and open my Bible, hoping that a Manna Verse would come to my rescue.

In a culture like ours nearly everyone has a few Bible verses in his memory bank. A fragment of the 23rd Psalm came to mind: ". . . he restoreth my soul . . ." While Demos was relating his story into the cassette I took advantage of this passage by repeating it a few times to myself under my breath.

And sure enough, a quiet infusion of strength came to me. It was Demos himself who finally looked at his watch and was surprised at the hour. So we said good night and I left.

With more than just a series of good notes, too. Because as I was putting on my pajamas by the light that came in from the street, so as not to wake Tib, I suddenly understood the experience I'd just had. I had stumbled onto an entirely *different* way God has of using His word. The verse I used was not a Manna Verse, coming right from the pages of the Bible, oddly fragile, like dew. This verse had been stored in my mind for years, ready, waiting. It seemed as if there were two distinct uses of Scripture; one was a Manna Verse, given by the Bible especially for today; the other was a memorized verse which perhaps could even be used over and over again.

A few days later, on our way home from Chicago, a winter storm forced long delays at O'Hare. At six o'clock in the morning we were sitting on a hard, plastic, vandal-proof bench in the airport waiting room. We were harrassed; we were exhausted. It was another situation where we needed a surge of strength. Perhaps the phrase from the 23rd Psalm would be helpful a second time? If so, this would be something new, because up until now the verses that were given as manna tended to go flat.

"Honey, do you remember what the Bible promises? 'He restoreth my soul . . .' Let's ask the Lord to give us that strength right now."

It was a beautiful thing watching the energy hidden in this word take control of our selves. We relaxed and waited, restored. When we did get on a flight we were refreshed. Even the crusty scrambled eggs served on the airline's best styrofoam seemed flavored with His caring.

Sometimes, then, God's provision *could* be stored, like weapons in an arsenal. These were valuable weapons, these Arsenal Verses. Surely I had some more stashed away! I remembered another which ministers were always using at the beginning of services. "I was glad when they said unto me, Let us go into the house of the Lord" (Psalm 122:1 KJV). And there was another which I remembered because it was carved in soot-streaked limestone above the gothic entrance to the seminary where my father taught in Louisville: "Lo, I am with you alway" (Matthew 28:20 KJV). I remembered these words because there was no "s" on "alway."

But at least they were part of my storehouse and sure enough, one day about a week after we came back from Chicago, I had a chance to depend on them. Liz, our last child, was about to leave home for college. Separation of any kind has always been difficult for me, no matter who leaves or for what reason. As I was beginning to catch signs of my separation anxieties I whispered aloud the words, "Lo, I am with you alway." In my heart I put the emphasis on I. And it helped. The words penetrated my fear and left me safe.

I was closing in on the difference between Manna Verses and Arsenal Verses.

* Manna Verses emphasize the oddly elusive nature of our relationship with God. We need to come to Him daily for a new supply of Himself. We can't capture Him, box Him. The poet Robert Frost once told Tib and me that he didn't like to try pinning down God with words. "It would be like pinning down a butterfly," he said. "If you do that you don't have a butterfly anymore."

* Arsenal Verses, paradoxically, emphasize the opposite. God's word is *also* imperishable, inexhaustible, eternal and it can be stored up just as swords can be stored in an arsenal.

* Manna Verses are evidence of God's moment-by-moment closeness. He is up-to-date on what happens in our lives, and says so by highlighting His involvement verse for each day of our lives.

* Arsenal Verses are evidence of God's unchangeability, of the permanent quality of His truth.

* To depend on either Manna or Arsenal Verses alone is to leave out an important part of God's provision.

* Both Manna and Arsenal Verses are of God's choosing. He will highlight a Manna Verse on a page, or bring to mind an Arsenal Verse which He knows will best fit our grip.

* God supplies the mystic energy in both experiences, too. The energy of a Manna Verse comes from the evidence of His caring, as when He tells us He is near, and loves us, or at times when He tells us that He disapproves of what we do. The energy of an Arsenal Verse comes from another kind of caring, as when we call on Him to do battle for us through the immense power of His word.

* Of course a Manna Verse can become an Arsenal Verse and vice versa. Any verse in the Bible can be either or both. When God gives a Manna Verse, if it has an unusual heft and balance and was given for a need that is likely to re-occur, why not memorize it and store it away?

6.

~~~~~~

Memorizing

BUT IT WAS right here, at this point of memorization, that I ran into real trouble.

When I became convinced that Arsenal Verses were a necessary part of my handling of problems, I made an inventory of the verses which I had at my disposal right then. Pitiful.

I've mentioned three. I could add another dozen, perhaps, but that exhausted my supply. I had not come from a tradition which emphasized learning the Bible. But that's not the real problem. The fact of the matter is that I have a very poor memory.

Scene: Tib and I are taking a course in French literature. Part of the classroom assignment is to learn short roles from Giraudoux's *Iphigénie*. Tib and I are to give a dialogue in class. I study my part diligently. Tib and I stand together in front of our fellow students. Tib delivers her opening line, then waits for me to pick up on her cue. She waits. And waits. She glances from me to the teacher in confusion. It is disaster for both of us, because I cannot remember a single word.

Scene: Greenwich Village, New York. It is many years later and I have been asked to take part in another play. Our then-teenaged son Scott has a friend, Chuck Nyren, who is a fledgling film producer. Chuck and Scott have written a screenplay. One part calls for a detective to enter a Greenwich Village apartment. He is wearing a raincoat. The detective—played by John Sherrill—is to shake water from his coat and speak the single line, "Well, I think we've got him."

This is such a simple scene there is no need to rehearse. Chuck has turned his floodlights on. The camera is rolling. Perhaps it is all the wires, the confusion, the sudden expectant quiet. I step through the door all right. I shake imaginary rainwater from my collar. I try to remember my line. The camera rolls. And rolls. And rolls . . .

How do you memorize if you have a leaky memory? Donn, when he was in high school, had brought home a book called, "How to Study." I got it out of the library, now, remembering that it had a chapter dealing with memorization.

There were, apparently, two keys. The first was repetition. The second was to spot whether you were a visual or oral learner. My basic orientation is visual. So I had the seemingly simple task of selecting Bible verses, writing them out and repeating them until they were mine.

Every day for several months I wrote out a new Bible verse on a 3 x 5 card and stuck it in my shirt pocket. Then, at random points through the day—while stopping at a traffic light, or sitting in a dentist's office, or waiting for the person I was calling to pick up the telephone—I would repeat the verse, then check my card to see how accurate I had been. Not very.

As the book suggested I developed a follow-up system. Keying the cyclical repetition to my desk calendar, I reviewed the verse every third day, then every seventh day, then every month. And sure enough I was anchoring a few verses. But still, if I am to be honest, many more got away from me.

And then, at last, I discovered a secret.

One day I was having lunch with a man who held the key to a story I was interested in. "I think maybe I can help you," the man said. "Let me give you my home phone number."

With that he took out of his pocket a pencil and paper and handed them to me. I picked up the pencil absently, but when the man gave me his ten-digit number I did not write it down.

"Have you got that?" he asked.

"Oh yes."

"Without writing it down?"

"Don't worry, I won't forget it."

The man took back his pencil commenting that he wished he had a good memory like mine.

A good memory! I had been telling myself that I could not recall a thing. Yet here I was confident that I could remember these ten numbers at will.

The key, I decided on reflection, was that my mind held on to things that were vital to me. I had very little trouble remembering the Manna Verses given to me most mornings, for I had learned from experience that these verses were going to be significant during the day. Since I knew they'd be important I could remember them without difficulty.

When it came to Arsenal Verses however I was in a different position. I had been trying to learn verses which only might *someday* turn out to be useful.

So I set about supplying myself with Arsenal Verses in a different way.

First, I limited my goal. I settled for an arsenal stocked

with just one hundred weapons in battle-ready shape. Surely that was manageable, even for me.

Second, with a few exceptions, I learned short selections, not only because they were easier to memorize but also because they worked better. Even when I learned longer passages, it was short *portions* of the passage that did the fighting.

Third, and most important, I learned verses that met specific, current needs. A relationship was in trouble; I was struggling with a destructive emotion; work was not going right; one of the children was taking a long car trip; my priorities were out of line; a friend was facing an operation . . . I knew that the Bible would speak to each such need. So as I met the situations I stopped and looked until I found a Bible verse to fit. Then I memorized that verse. (In King James English, usually: I find it easier to remember because of the almost scannable sentence structure.)

At last I was under way. The hundred verses were not easy for me to learn, but learn them I did. They are mine forever now and I use them all the time. I've made a list of my particular hundred in the back of this book, although of course each person's battlegrounds and therefore choice of weapons will be different.

But there was one dynamic still to be explored, in the art of using these Manna and Arsenal Verses. And that was how best to release the power that lay coiled within them waiting to be used.

7.

The Partnership of Power

BOTH MANNA AND Arsenal Verses have the power to alter situations. But that power remains latent until it is released, as I discovered one evening:

There is a popular theory that a strange "pecking order" exists among people, similar to an order which can be found in a barnyard. A dominant rooster pecks another. He pecks a hen; she pecks on still another hen below her in the order. And so it goes right down to the bottom. I've observed this in myself. For reasons that resist understanding, I am below some people in the human pecking order, and above others.

I noticed it, for instance, one evening when Tib and I were visiting a writer who lives in nearby Connecticut. I admired Philip too much to be at ease with him. It was one of those excessive admirations that left me a little in awe. Philip was *too* talented, too surefooted, too witty. He chose other giants for his friends, which left me out.

Now we were moving into the dining room where Philip's ancient housekeeper (naturally, I found this setup the epitome of glamour) had prepared a welcoming meal.

As we were settling down I remembered something. Weeks ago in another context altogether I had stored away a short Arsenal Verse, from Acts 10:34 (KJV), "God is no respecter of persons . . ." God shows no partiality. He plays no favorites. There the Arsenal Verse lay, but that's as far as I got. Just then the housekeeper arrived with the tureen of soup, my attention was distracted.

Until, that is, just after supper when Philip took us for a stroll along his own private lakefront. I was in the process of feeling that this was surely the most favored of all writer's havens when *again* the verse from Acts 10:34 came to mind.

"Wait a minute," I said to myself while Tib carried the conversation. "Just *having* that verse isn't enough." It lay there, I went on thinking, filled with wonderful latent power, but just possessing it did not automatically release that power into my awkwardness. I had to go into partnership, as it were, with God. I had to *do* something, actively take a step, in order to release the dynamic potential within that verse. Otherwise, I suppose, if God did everything automatically, He would be violating my free will. My will had to be involved in order to complete the circuit.

"God is no respecter of persons," I said.

"What's that, John?" said Philip. "You'll do what?"

". . . uh . . . excuse me . . ."

But Philip was already off again following his own thoughts. *God is no respecter of persons,* I said again, pronouncing the words with my lips, as if saying them aloud. God does not see Philip as "higher" or "lower" than I am. God is not partial. Philip is just Philip, with his own talents and problems. Philip is Philip with weaknesses and strong points. He is Philip and I am John.

Well I can report that a change began that same night. I felt more at ease with the man. Tib did not have to do all the talking anymore. And ever since then it has been far easier to get along with myself when I'm around Philip. Later the miracle occurred again in a relationship where I myself was "higher" on that strange and artificial pecking order. I found I could break the order down with the same Arsenal Verse no matter where I stood on the scale. I could be just plain John. But again I had to say the verse aloud or as close to aloud as the social situation permitted.

What exactly was happening here? I recalled how a Manna Verse came to my aid when I was tempted to cheat on a royalty report; I had repeated the protecting verse aloud on that occasion. I remembered when I sat down with Stan, my bachelor friend whose creativity was bottled up; there too I had spoken the Bible verse aloud. Was there something special in actually speaking a verse out? It was the American poetess Emily Dickinson who said,

A word is dead
When it is said,
Some say.
I say it just
Begins to live
That day.

Was speaking forth the creative principle that converted latent power into actual power?

* "And God *said*, Let there be light: and there was light" (Genesis 1:3 KJV). The saying forth came before the manifestation.

* ". . . if you confess *with your lips* that Jesus is Lord . . . you will be saved" (Romans 10:9 RSV). To "confess" in this sense means to "say with" God. When I confess God's word I am pronouncing His own word with Him.

* And that spoken-out word had God's promise of effec-

tiveness. " . . . so shall my word be that *goes forth from my mouth;* it shall not return to me empty, but it shall accomplish that which I purpose . . ." (Isaiah 55:11 RSV).

* "The centurion answered and said, Lord, I am not worthy that thou shouldest come under my roof: but *speak* the word only, and my servant shall be healed" (Matthew 8:8 KJV). The centurion knew that Jesus had the power, *provided* it was sent forth.

* "For he *spake, and it was done;* he commanded, and it stood fast" (Psalm 33:9 KJV).

All of these examples are epitomised in Jesus' own experience in the wilderness.

My daily lectionary readings had brought Tib and me to Luke 4 where Jesus is tempted in the wilderness. Three times in a row He faced His trials by using Scripture in this same Speaking-Forth Principle. He showed how to turn a Latent Power verse into Actual Power. From His store of Scripture, He exploded Satan's luring suggestions by aiming one perfect word at the argument, then releasing its incredible power by speaking it forth.

Of all the principles I had encountered to date, this was perhaps the most important.

The Spirit took the first step in this cooperative effort by singling out verses to be used. He alone knew the complexities that surrounded a situation. He highlighted a passage or brought a memorized verse freshly to mind.

But then an act on my part was required.

I had to take this verse and apply it.

I had to speak it—preferably aloud—into the situation.

But when I did, Jesus' temptations promised, miracles of power ensued.

8.

Counterfeit Suggestions for Power

SOMETHING WAS bothering me.

What was there in the account of Jesus' temptation in the wilderness that I had missed? I got out the Bible and re-read the last part of the story, where Satan set Jesus on a pinnacle of the temple and said to Him:

"If you are the Son of God, throw yourself down from here; for it is written,
  'He will give his angels charge of you,
  to guard you,'
  and
  'On their hands they will bear you up,
  lest you strike your foot against a stone.'"
And Jesus answered him, "It is said, 'You shall not tempt the Lord your God.'"

Luke 4:9–12 RSV

Jesus wasn't the only one speaking forth passages of Scripture in this account.

Satan did too.

Satan spoke Scripture accurately and even at greater

length than did Jesus. So there was something wrong with assuming that just because a Bible verse is spoken, it is necessarily a Power Verse, infused with the Holy Spirit's vitality.

Even while I was thinking about this, I remembered another encounter with the Luke 4 reading, years earlier. I recalled the experience vividly, as if I were living it over again, a traumatic little event that happened when our son Scott was fifteen.

On that morning Scott was not in the house: he was on an overnight camping trip. Tib and I were having breakfast when we received a phone call from a neighbor with the news that he had seen Scott, a few days earlier, driving our family car down a nearby country lane. Was he sure it was *Scott?* Yes. When was this again? Two, three days ago. Well, thanks for letting us know.

Tib and I sat there letting our eggs grow cold as we tried to come to grips with our anger and puzzlement. What were we going to do? Scott had been so anxious to drive that I had occasionally talked him through the controls of a car, but always with the explicit instructions that he was never, never to touch those controls unless I were actually with him.

Now he had deliberately disobeyed. On one point Tib and I were united: we had to have a definite plan of action ready by the time Scott arrived home at five.

This whole misadventure was taking place in the early days of our experiments with the Bible, so I found myself wondering if we could find a good Scriptural guideline. Sure enough, the shadow of a verse came to mind.

Wasn't there an instruction that said you were not to get your children angry? I got the concordance down from its shelf and looked up the word *children.* Sure enough there was my verse:

And, ye fathers, provoke not your children to wrath: but bring them up in the nurture and admonition of the Lord.
Ephesians 6:4 KJV

Well, that seemed clear enough. We should not provoke Scott to wrath. That would mean going easy on him I supposed . . . Good. I was relieved. I never have been good at confrontations, because I am afraid of my own anger. Perhaps I could just pray with the boy and show him God's way.

Yet I was uncomfortable. Just the week before I'd heard a sermon on discipline. Hadn't the preacher quoted *another* Scripture verse to the effect that although chastening was never easy to go through, it produced good results.

Uneasily—because I didn't really want to find it— I riffled through the concordance again until I came to the word *discipline* and shortly I found this second reference too. I turned to the chapter in Hebrews and read this unwelcome passage:

For the moment all discipline seems painful rather than pleasant; later it yields the peaceful fruit of righteousness to those who have been trained by it.
Hebrews 12:11 RSV

According to this verse I was to have no hesitation in disciplining Scott for this breach of rules. Hard as the correction was it would later produce "peaceful fruit."

My heart sank. If I followed this verse I couldn't avoid the showdown.

So I was confused. The verses seemed to give opposite instructions. Throughout the day Tib and I talked over our dilemma but we couldn't come up with any good way to tell which verse we should follow. It wasn't that one was the word of God, while the other was secular wisdom: both were Scriptural. It wasn't even that one was from the New Testament and the other from the Old: both were from the Epistles.

The day was almost over. In an hour Scott would be coming home and I did not know how to face him.

"Lord, it's Your guideline we're trying to use," I said aloud. "You'll just have to solve the dilemma."

Tib began putting together a casserole. I headed out to pick late September tomatoes. But I had not even reached the door before I let out a hoot.

"Tib! I think I remember something!"

I came back to the kitchen, got out the Bible and opened it to Luke 4, where the lectionary had brought me just that morning. I read aloud Satan's words to Jesus:

". . . If you are the Son of God, throw yourself down from here; for it is written,
  'He will give his angels charge of you,
  to guard you,'
  and
  'On their hands they will bear you up,
  lest you strike your foot against a stone.'"
And Jesus answered him, "It is said, 'You shall not tempt the Lord your God.'"

"Look," I said patting the page. "Jesus has already gone through this for us. Whenever we have conflicting voices, two opposite solutions suggested by Scripture, we should remember that *there can be nothing wrong with the verses themselves.* They are both the word of God. The problem isn't with the word. The problem is with *who is doing the suggesting.*"

We were off and running. Of course! This would explain how some of the most heinous acts in the world— the Inquisition, the witch hunts of Salem, modern-day

lunatic murders "because the Bible told me to do it"—
could have been based on Scripture. Scripture had been
involved all right. Who, though, had suggested that particular passage in that particular life context?

"That's tricky," Tib worried. "Who are *we* to decide
that one verse comes from God and another from Satan?"
Yet that too could be Satan's counterfeit argument. Because right there before us we had our model. Jesus had
identified the suggester, and so should we.

How had Jesus known? There were several criteria I
could think of:

* What were the *long-term* results of following one
verse rather than the other. Satan is likely to hold out
short-term appeal.

* Galatians 5:22 lists the Fruit of the Spirit. Which
verse, if followed, would produce that fruit?

* Would one verse leave us in a minute-by-minute de-
pendence on God while another left us forging ahead on
our own?

* And most important of all: What does our discernment say? Discerning of spirits, as described in 1 Corinthians 12:10, is one of the most important of the gifts of
the Spirit. Whose spirit is operating when a verse is suggested? Jesus knew instantly, and every Christian has
access to that same knowledge.

Which spirit was behind the suggestions we faced now?
Was it the Holy Spirit? Or was it Satan's spirit? I thought
I knew but I wanted to test my reaction against Tib's.
We prayed together, "Father, we know that Satan can
urge Scripture on us. But with Your help, we won't let

him do it. Give both of us, Lord, a clear discernment, we ask. Which of these verses has been suggested by You?"

And suddenly it was all over. We knew! There was no doubt which passage had come from Jesus. The one that told us to chastise, even though the chastisement would be temporarily grievous. The opposite, ducking the discipline for fear that we would stir up wrath—Scott's or my own—that course wouldn't be right *in this case.*

When Scott came home a half an hour later we were prepared. I set the boy down and left no doubt in his mind what I thought about his driving episode. Scott was subdued, all the more so when I said that he was grounded; he had to come home immediately after school for a month. Of course Scott was angry; he tried every trick in the trade-of-boyhood to get around our decision. But we had going for us something that was rock solid, a quickened verse of Scripture that the Lord had given us just for this occasion.

And in the strength of this power we were able to maintain our firmness, even when it was hard on everyone. Scott got terribly bored after a week of hanging around the house. If it had not been for our verse—which I repeated over and over to myself—I would have been tempted to back away from the discipline because Tib and I were about to lose our minds with Scott's wandering about the house, or sitting at the yellow breakfast table drawing pictures with drops of spilled milk, or playing the same song over and over on the stereo.

But instead of weakening I encouraged Scott to help me rebuild a chest of drawers in my shop. Scott had never been interested in working with his hands. He was in the drama club at school, he was a songwriter, a guitar player, a spinner of tales. But out of that time together in my shop came a surprise. Scott had a flair for using tools. He was intent as we used auger and miter box together. He seemed really interested when I told him which hand-made tool, which file and plane had come down to us from his west Texas great-grandfather.

Today Scott is struggling to make his way as a musician. But he supports himself and his wife and their baby daughter with carpentry. I often wonder if his interest dates back to the choice Tib and I had to make between two Bible verses which seemed to contradict each other. One was a true Power Verse, the other was a Counterfeit Power Verse. Only one was right in this *particular situation*. The problem wasn't with the word, the problem was with who suggested the word for right now. One verse had been truly quickened; the other was only dormant, stored in the Bible, ready and waiting for the Spirit to bring it to life at another time and place. Satan had tried to take the dormant verse and make it *appear* to be infused with the Spirit's power for this situation.

One verse left God in charge.

Only that one would do.

9.

Getting Specific—
Even Though I'd Rather Not

Interlude

BY NOW I COULD see that it is possible to make friends with the Bible. I could bring myself to it and expect the Spirit to talk to me through its pages. It was a mystic communion where God would support, defend, correct.

But of course making friends with the Bible didn't happen in a vacuum. It took place in terms of a real life —in this case, my own. The life I've described so far has dealt with homey matters such as with dogs and cars and real estate cheats.

But there were other areas that couldn't be handled in a day. Darker, more unyielding areas that I brought with me into my Christian life from before I saw Jesus in that hospital room. Jarring and jolting terrain that kept throwing me off balance. Ground which I was afraid to talk about, because I feared I would be scandalizing some people, or causing others to say, "What's he trying to do, be a little tin saint?"

The point is that, here too, the experiences I am going to describe were my own. My problems were in the areas of sex, and competition, and over-indulgence, and fear. Someone else's will be different, but I suspect that we would share in common the fact that we have, in our make-up, stubborn fortresses whose lords don't give up easily.

The Bible had proven itself a friend in simpler, day-to-day problems. Would it also prove a companion-at-arms against these tougher enemies?

Problems Are Temptations

As I began to explore this question I found myself being drawn again and again to one portion of the Bible, the Temptation of Jesus. At first I thought this was just a personal preference. But then I began to suspect that the Temptation was not pulling me to itself just because I had testings of my own.

Perhaps the Temptation was God's Master Plan for Handling Problems?

If so, I was still missing something in that reading. So one bright morning with the sunlight streaming through our livingroom window, I sat down again trying to come to grips with the elusive deeper meaning to the Temptation story. I read carefully:

> And Jesus, full of the Holy Spirit, returned from the Jordan, and was led by the Spirit for forty days in the wilderness, tempted by the devil. And he ate nothing in those days; and when they were ended, he was hungry. The devil said to him, "If you are the Son of God, command this stone to become bread."
>
> And Jesus answered him, "It is written, 'Man shall not live by bread alone.'"
>
> And the devil took him up, and showed him all the kingdoms of the world in a moment of time, and said to him, "To you I will give all this authority and their glory; for it has been delivered to me, and I give it to whom I will. If you, then, will worship me, it shall all be yours."

And Jesus answered him, "It is written,
  'You shall worship the Lord your God, and
  him only shall you serve.' "
And he took him to Jerusalem, and set him on the pinnacle of the temple, and said to him, "If you are the Son of God, throw yourself down from here; for it is written,
  'He will give his angels charge of you,
   to guard you,'
and
  'On their hands they will bear you up,
   lest you strike your foot against a stone.' "
And Jesus answered him, "It is said, 'You shall not tempt the Lord your God.' " And when the devil had ended every temptation, he departed from him until an opportune time.
And Jesus returned in the power of the Spirit into Galilee . . .

Luke 4:4–14 RSV

A remarkable thing happened to me as I followed this account. *Two* different verses were highlighted.

The first was, "And Jesus, full of the Holy Spirit, returned from the Jordan, and was led by the Spirit for forty days in the wilderness, tempted by the devil."

The second came thirteen verses later. "And Jesus returned in the power of the Spirit into Galilee . . ."

I copied the two verses out in longhand, and it was in doing this that I noticed a striking similarity between them:

Jesus went *into* the wilderness full of the Spirit. He came *out of* the wilderness still in the Spirit.

Jesus remained in the Spirit, no matter what happened. This, I recalled, was the crucial signal by which John the Baptist could know that he had found Christ. John was to watch for one man on whom the Holy Spirit would descend and remain (John 1:33). Descend and *remain.* No other man in history had lived in such a way that the

Spirit descended on him, and stayed with him always.

To stay in the Spirit—I was sure of it now—was the real problem Jesus faced in the wilderness.

The wilderness did not offer three different temptations as I'd always thought. It offered one. A single temptation: in the shape of different problems, to be sure, but a single testing just the same. The problems were in the area of His physical body (when He was hungry after a prolonged fast); in the area of His soul—His mind, emotions, affections (in questions involving His work); and in the area of His spirit (when He was offered a spiritual shortcut).

For Jesus, the problems were all temptations. Each had a common denominator. Each tried, with its particular pressures, to lure Him away from the Spirit.

What does it mean to be "in the Spirit"?

When I tried to communicate this to Tib, though, I ran into a problem. "What do you mean by 'in the Spirit'?" she asked.

"Well . . . you know . . . in the *Spirit*."

"I couldn't tell you what the phrase means, though. Can you?"

"No."

So, before I could go any further, I had to come to grips more precisely with this term. Paul says we should "Walk in the Spirit . . ." (Galatians 5:16 KJV). John said that he was ". . . in the Spirit" on the Lord's day (Revelation 1:10 KJV). Jesus returned from the wilderness ". . . in the power of the Spirit . . ." (Luke 4:14 KJV). What was the experience conveyed in this phrase?

I had a hint from my own life. After my conversion, and later after my Baptism in the Holy Ghost I was, for a few weeks or months, palpably "in the Spirit." That is, I lived for a time in an exhilarating realm. Life was aglow. People were aglow. For a short while I was living so far above my problems that I couldn't see them.

But we don't live forever in such a state, not here on earth. I came down from my heaven and began to realize that problems were still here. That first-blush euphoria bore the same relationship to the *walk* in the Spirit that a honeymoon bears to *marriage*.

So I had to dig some more, and I did so by asking friends who might have hard experience behind their answers, what they included in the concept, "in the Spirit." Here is what I gleaned:

* To be in the Spirit is to become conscious, for a higher percentage of time, of God's continuing presence in our lives.

* To be in the Spirit is to be in the flow of His vital life and power.

* To be in the Spirit involves a quality of living, because the Fruit of the Spirit is growing:

> . . . the fruit of the Spirit is love, joy, peace, patience, kindness, goodness, faithfulness, gentleness, self control . . .
>
> Galatians 5:22, 23 RSV

* To be in the Spirit is to exist in a different realm where miracle is not a surprise.

* There, in the realm of the Spirit, we have available the Gifts of the Spirit, ours to use as problems and opportunities present themselves.

> For to one is given by the Spirit the word of wisdom; to another the word of knowledge by the same Spirit; to another faith by the same Spirit; to another the gifts of healing by the same Spirit; to another the working of miracles; to another prophecy; to another discerning of spirits; to another divers kinds of tongues; to another the interpretation of tongues.
>
> 1 Corinthians 12:8–10 KJV

* To be in the Spirit is to be in the Kingdom of God for a given moment of time. Gordon Lyle, an investment counselor from Westport, Connecticut, sums it up this way. You are in the kingdom—in the Spirit—when you are:

> . . . most fully yourself
> . . . doing what the Father wants you to be doing
> . . . using the tools He wants you to use
> . . . when He wants you to use them
> . . . where He wants you to be
> . . . for His own purposes.

All this was inherent in the expression "in the Spirit."

No wonder Satan wanted to seduce Jesus away from this position. All of the temptations he threw at Jesus were aimed at that same goal. Satan took problems and shaped them into temptations. Each problem became a red herring trying to attract His attention. Satan forever tempted Him (as he tempts us all) to move out of the Spirit by turning toward the problem instead of toward the Father.

I wondered if I would ever be able to handle problems the way Jesus did. Could I learn to treat all problems as the single temptation to move out from the Spirit?

My problems themselves might, or might not, go away. That, apparently, was not Jesus' main concern. The issue was not to solve problems, or to avoid them, but to handle them in the Spirit.

And the way Jesus did this, without exception, was through Scripture.

10.

Red Herring No. 1:
Physical Problems

JESUS WAS HUNGRY. Satan tempted Him to meet this physical problem by commanding the stones which lay around Him so abundantly to be turned into bread.

Real as it was, the problem with hunger was an issue which was meant to distract. Satan tried to get Jesus to focus on His physical needs, but Jesus saw the ruse as a temptation to shift His gaze away from the face of the Father. That was the real problem: staying in constant touch with the Father.

Jesus handled this temptation by depending on Scripture. Against the suggestion of Satan, He immediately used the word of God. It was the only weapon He used, even though He could have turned to other powers available to Him—miracles, angels, prayer. Of all His resources He chose to lean only on the Scripture given to Him specifically for this occasion.

I came down the stairs in our little, somewhat-Tudor house in Oxford, England, determined not to let my anxiety show. Tib had set breakfast in our "sunny" living room. Actually, the sun was only wishfulness, for the July skies were colored orange-gray again by smog from the industrial belt that surrounded Oxford. But I wasn't going to let that get at me today.

Tib and I were living in England on a year-long writing assignment. Only our youngest, Liz, was with us. Scott was out of college, married now, and living with his wife Meg in New Hampshire; Donn was at the University of Madrid in Spain; he would be joining us here next month.

We certainly had every reason to believe that we were where the Lord wanted us. He had provided this house, for example, when real estate agents said none were available.

He had even provided a gardener. The yard around our house was what had first attracted us, but we had not suspected what it meant to have an *English* garden! Constant blooming we soon discovered comes with constant grooming. Between our lack of time and lack of know-how the lovely grounds became shaggier and shaggier.

So we began to ask neighbors if they knew of a local gardener. General laughter greeted the question. We were thinking of an England of years ago, we were told. It was practically impossible to find a gardener today. One woman did have an old putterer-arounder, but he was 93 and about to retire. Another knew of a lawn service, high price, poor quality. By every standard the answer to our question—and our prayers—was No.

Then one day there was a knock at the front door. At first I thought the well-groomed man standing at our threshold was a door-to-door salesman; we lived on a busy street.

"Can I help you?" Unencouragingly.

"I don't know," the man said. "Do you need a gardener? I'm looking for work."

Samuel Mitchum, incredibly, wanted just the eight hours a week which our garden needed. His charges were reminiscent of the old days: the equivalent of two American dollars an hour. It turned out that he was an itinerant preacher spending this season in Oxfordshire. Mr. Mitchum did not agree with the way the government was spending his tax money, so he worked for the number of hours that put him just under the minimum income level before taxation. The balance of his time was spent in street evangelism.

So there was no doubt in our mind that we were where He wanted us to be. If we needed encouragement on that score, He was giving it to us.

Yet as I came down the last stair that morning and headed into the living room for my favorite breakfast of kippers-and-poached, Tib took one look at me and asked what was wrong. Nothing. Was I sure? Certainly.

With an excellent show of cheerfulness, it seemed to me, I left our house and started my morning walk down to the office. Our house did not have enough room for Tib and me both to have work space there so I had rented a room in a private home in central Oxford. The idea of walking the mile and a half each way each day seemed a good one at first. But I soon discovered why Oxford has a reputation for bad air. Although the city is best known for its university, Oxford is also a major automobile manufacturing center. Convoys of transport trucks move in and out, spitting their choking diesel foulness into the air. Because Oxford sits in a shallow valley the septic air cannot escape. I quickly discovered that trying to get to my office by the main road meant fighting diesels all the way. I would have abandoned walking altogether if I had not discovered the canal.

Hidden behind a row of houses in Oxford is a stretch

of old barge canal, dating back to the days before the railroad. The canal, used now mostly for holiday barges, flowed right past the backyard of my office. So each morning I walked the towpath, past old boatyards and lush playing fields where schoolboys were intent on their soccer games.

Now, on this morning when I had told Tib nothing was wrong, I walked along my towpath trying to keep as calm as the swans that slid along the water beside me. But I wasn't calm. I tried humming. That was a mistake. Three bars into the melody and I had to stop, clear my throat, try again, stop again. The panic that rode my spine and exploded in my brain was not to be stilled by a song.

For persistent hoarseness is one of the classic danger signs of cancer.

I had been trying for two months to ignore the signals. If you paid attention to every little cough . . . But programming my thoughts didn't work. My mind insisted on snapping back to my two previous cancer battles, and that morning as I passed a humpbacked bridge on the canal I admitted at last that I was afraid.

And I knew the name of the fear, too. Pain. Not death, but pain. Ironically, although after Marc Hall's prayers at our church my surgeon had found only dried up nodules on my neck, although the cancer had been healed by the Lord, still I had very nearly died on the operating table when my lungs collapsed under anesthesia. Now, I relived the memory of waking up in the recovery room so pierced by pain that I clawed my way out of bed, pulling at all the doctors' wires and tubes. Nurses dashed up, pushed me down, inserted hypodermics. As I went out, I was saying to myself, "Never. I won't go through this again."

So that July morning I went to my office in Oxford, all

right, but I didn't get much done. Instead of working I stared out the window at the slender vacation barges that slipped past, painted in swirling gypsy colors. Eleven thirty came. Good, it was time for lunch. I walked down to the corner and ordered a leisurely Pakistani meal. No reason to hurry. When I returned I was drowsy and decided on a short snooze. I put my head down on the table, then awoke to doodle for a while. Then it was time to go home.

This became my pattern. Although I had put a name to my fears, I still did not worry aloud. I did not tell Tib. I did not go to the doctor, who might confirm what I suspected. I did drop into church on my way home from work one day but the empty and cold sanctuary seemed to capture the sound of my cough and throw it back at me.

I shunned Scripture as effectively as I avoided Tib. I hid from both with the only successful playacting I had ever achieved. Or at least I thought it was successful, because both Tib and God let me go my lonesome way for a while. I continued to talk to Tib about the weather and what I had for lunch, and plans for meeting Donn's plane when he came in from Spain in a few days. It was talk without communicating.

It was the same with the Bible. Tib and I did continue to read selections from the morning lectionary, but I discovered, those days, how easy it is to read the Bible and not hear it at all.

What I did do, in contrast, was to step out of the Spirit altogether. I disappeared into excellent British television and into wine. A sallow-faced man kept a Wine and Spirits Shoppe a few blocks from our home and it was the rare evening that did not see me stopping for a bottle of claret. Or so.

Then one night Tib and I went to the Bear Hotel in Woodstock, just outside of Oxford. The Bear is our favorite hotel in the world and that night we splurged by ordering the house specialty, Blenheim partridge. It was served to us by soft-voiced waiters in red jackets. Candles burned. Shining silver stretched away on three sides of our plates. And of course, the sommelier kept our glasses filled.

Toward the middle of the meal, Tib leaned forward.

"I don't think you're playing fair with me."

I took a bite of the partridge and ate in silence. Tib wouldn't help me out. She said nothing more. Finally, I spoke the words I should have said months ago.

"You're right. I'm scared."

"What is it John?"

"Well," I cleared my throat once again and took another large swallow of claret. "Well, for a couple of months I've had this hoarseness in my throat and trouble swallowing and it's getting worse."

It all came out in a rush. Once I had started, I found myself telling Tib about the first day I'd noticed it, walking beside my canal. I told her about the empty, workless days, about my determination to carry the fear by myself. Tib's dinner sat on her plate, untouched from the moment I had started my confession.

". . . no, it's excellent . . . it's just that I'm not hungry." Tib was explaining to the head waiter.

"You see I was right," I said as the waiter left us, "I shouldn't have dumped this on your shoulders. I want you to *promise* you won't tell anyone else. Not the kids. Or our mothers. Not even the prayer group."

As far as I can recall, only once in our lives has Tib simply ignored my wishes. That same evening, without telling me of course, she wrote to our prayer group back in New York, telling them exactly what was happening.

At Tib's insistence I began making inquiries, trying to find the best head-and-neck specialist in the United Kingdom. We asked our friend Edward England, who directs the Religious Book Division of Hodder and Stoughton; and we asked our friend Ray Cripps, the first publisher and editor of *Guideposts* in Britain. Encouragingly, they both came up with the same name. The specialist, when we reached him, knew my surgeon in New York, and agreed to see me in a week.

"A week!"

"I'm sorry," the doctor said, "I'm going to be on the Continent until then. Of course, we could refer you to someone else . . ."

"All right," I said into the phone. "I'll be there." The hour was fixed for eleven o'clock Wednesday morning a week away.

Suddenly we had seven days of hard waiting on our hands. We'd originally planned a vacation during this time. Donn and I have birthdays on August 1 and August 2. Donn was flying in tomorrow from Spain. Liz' school year was over. We had planned to celebrate all these occasions at once by taking a week-long do-it-your-self trip on the Thames in a small river launch.

"Do you think we should just go ahead?" Tib asked as we drove to the airport to pick up Donn.

I shrugged. Why not? I didn't think I could take a week of just waiting around. We also discussed whether or not to bring Donn and Liz in on our problem. After all, we didn't know yet that the fear was based on reality. But was reality the criterion? Or was the fact that I was afraid, by itself, enough.

Next morning our gear was stowed aboard *Wingo*, with its tiny galley and its four narrow bunks and its mini-deck aft. The launch was snugly moored to a tree at the boatyard on the River Thames at Oxford. I'd had very little experience with boats, but nonetheless Donn and Liz and Tib and I climbed aboard with great confidence. After all, the owner himself had seemed satisfied a little while ago when he had taken us out to show me the controls. On that trial run, once we were underway, he let me handle the boat. It seemed surprisingly nimble—the zig-zag wake we left behind us did puzzle the owner a bit.

The Thames is very narrow and rapid at Oxford. A maelstrom, so to say. It apparently didn't seem dangerous to the young men from the university who were out in their punts, moving so nonchalantly over the water. Nor had the river presented a problem to the owner when he swung *Wingo* around neatly to moor her to this tree. He turned the keys over to me with the encouraging remark, "There. Nothing to it."

Even now he seemed satisfied as he waited on the bank a discreet distance away, watching as Donn stood at the bowline, answered my forefinger-to-thumb high sign with a salute. And then Donn cast off.

I eased the throttle forward, nosed the boat out into that current and promptly found myself swinging in circles.

I caught sight of the owner who was running to the edge of the bank whirling his arms counterclockwise and shouting. "Port! Hard to port!" Port? Donn fended off a startled young man who was out skulling, then I lurched forward once more and at last we were off. Headed downstream. Liz pointed *upstream*. "Dad, I thought we were going that way." I mumbled something and kept going. Not in the direction we had originally planned, to be sure. But I wasn't going to correct that mistake now.

All that afternoon the rigors of learning how to handle *Wingo* were so time-consuming that we had no opportunity to bring up the subject of cancer.

But at last it was evening. We moored against a steep, chisled bank along the Thames. Supper was over. A rare, warm evening let us linger outdoors on the rear deck. A swan family, father and mother and three cygnets, sailed by not even acknowledging us with a turn of the head. In the distance across the tableland farms of Oxfordshire, a country churchbell sounded. It was the right time.

I told the kids. I told them about the hoarseness, the fears, the loneliness. I told them of the upcoming visit to the specialist and of our hopes that it would be a good report. Tib confessed she had written the prayer group, and I found I was glad. Tib even had a reply from our friend Jean Nardozzi which she read now. Jean said a lot of people were praying for us; she chided me for keeping my fear secret and urged us to stay close to the Bible.

"Then let's do it," said Donn.

Tib got out the lectionary. I explained to the kids where I was now in this adventure with the Bible, how before I started running scared I had been learning to let the Bible speak to me.

"Maybe that could happen now," Liz suggested. I hoped so. Tib and Donn and Liz read while I listened. Tib started with a Psalm. Nothing. Then Donn read a passage from Jeremiah. Nothing. Then Liz began the eighth chapter of Romans. Still nothing was happening. I wondered if I was in for another of those times when the Bible would not speak, when suddenly there it was. How well I remember Liz' clear, soft, still slightly tearful voice. She read, "For you did not receive the spirit of slavery to fall back into fear . . ." (Romans 8:15 rsv).

I sat up straighter. That was *my* verse! I asked Liz to read it again. As she spoke I realized that this was *exactly* what a consuming fear produced, a spirit of slavery. I was bound by it and wanted release. I told the kids what I was finding out about converting Latent Power into

Actual Power, by speaking forth a verse. Then, there on
our boat I put into practice the principle Jesus taught in
the wilderness.

"All right, Lord," I said. "I'm going to move to the attack. I know this verse is mine, and I take it up as the only
weapon I need. I claim this as Your own voice speaking
a fact. 'I did not receive the spirit of slavery to fall back
into fear, but I have received the spirit of sonship.' Lord,
I speak that fact forth."

To say that I had no problem staying in God's presence
after that would of course be simplistic. I did have bolts
of fear thrown at me and the fear did grab my attention,
diverting it from God. The difference was that now I also
had a weapon to throw against the fear, allowing me to
move back quickly into the Spirit. Every time I was at-
tacked, I did one thing only, and I did it instantly. I
stated my fact. *For you did not receive the spirit of slavery to fall back into fear, but you received the spirit of
sonship.* I thanked the Lord for that fact. That's all I did.
Nothing more. No arguing, no analyzing. I just said that
Power Verse into the fear, and it went away. Temporarily,
but it did go away. When it returned, I repeated my de-
fense in childlike simplicity.

All I can say is that the rest of our week on the Thames
was almost one hundred percent sheer, abandoned joy.
We laughed. We overate. We moored the boat and went
on long walks. At the last possible minute we headed
back.

The boat owner was there waiting for us. He did not
try to hide his astonishment that we had made the trip
without accident.

"Congratulations!" he said as he pocketed the ignition
key a little too quickly, it seemed to me, and wrung my
hand.

Yes, we all agreed, it had been a marvelous trip. I did

not know what the result of the doctor's examination was going to be next day. But I'd reached that wonderful place where—at least as far as this situation was concerned—staying in the Spirit did not depend on my problem's being solved.

It was Wednesday. Eleven in the morning. All of us —Tib and Donn and Liz and I—were sitting in the uncomfortable waiting room of London's ancient, red brick prison-like hospital which specializes in cancer and related conditions.

My name was called.

Two hours of swallowing strange material, being strapped on a machine and turned upside down, submitting to thumps and whacks and tongue depressors and blood specimens and X-rays and tests I couldn't fathom at all.

"Would you all like to be together when I give you the report?" the doctor asked at the end of all of this.

"Yes."

So the doctor took us into his office, set us down in a circle . . . and then smiled.

"I know how worried you must be. But I have the best of reports for you. I can find absolutely nothing wrong."

A too-good-to-be-true silence.

"You live in Oxford don't you?" the doctor asked.

"That's right."

"And for how long?"

I counted back. "Eight months."

"It generally takes four for throat symptoms to appear." The doctor shook his head. "It's the Oxford air. I shouldn't be surprised if that city's air isn't the worst in the world. Oxford will make the healthiest of us cough, and you seem to be unusually susceptible. You're suffering from simple twentieth-century pollution."

We stopped at the first restaurant we came to. It had sidewalk tables. There we celebrated with a victory dinner, but even as we ate I knew we had already celebrated the real victory, aboard *Wingo*. As I was enjoying myself I got to thinking. My physical problem had been in the area of health. But it could have been in any area that touches our physical lives: overweight, or trying to get along on too little money, or even just some feature of our appearance we don't like. All are red herring problems in that they demand so much attention they can take us away from what should be the focus of our lives. The problems are real, but they mask a greater problem: in Satan's hands they become temptations to take our eyes off God.

I wish I could say that the principles I had been learning so painfully now carried over automatically to the next problem-temptation I faced.

Unfortunately that is not the case.

11.

~~~~~~

Red Herring No. 2:
Problems in Our Work

JESUS HAD WORK to do. Important work which had been given Him by the Father.

But this very fact gave the devil an opportunity to attack. Satan knew that he could make this work go faster and—to all appearances—better. He could effectively and efficiently deliver to Jesus all the kingdoms of the earth. Satan also knew that unless Jesus used his, Satan's, methods He would reach only a few people during His lifetime. That achievement would certainly not appear to be very spectacular.

"The way your work is done," Satan whispers, "is not so important as results. Let me help you and you'll get more done. Keep your eye on the outcome. That's all that really matters."

We all face this red herring of achievement. And it is especially subtle when our work is good, valuable, helpful to others. A woman is raising children; what could be more important? A man's company hires hundreds of people, scores of families depend for their livelihood on landing a certain contract. Still another has a "ministry"

given him by God Himself. We often can honestly per-
suade ourselves that the success of our work is more im-
portant than how we achieve it.

In my own case, Tib and I were writing books which
we hoped were important. The methods we used? Well,
it's true that the methods were hurting us. But then . . .

We have good friends, Frank and Claire Coffin, who
own a home on Nantucket Island. Every now and then
Tib and I will go there off season for a few days of work
away from the telephone. In the very early spring when
it is still cold, before the summer residents come, Frank
and Claire's house is so isolated that we can go for days
with the low-hovering harriers as our only companions.

I was at the Coffins' place now. I had come alone this
time because, in addition to a project for *Guideposts*, I
had another kind of work to do. I'd come armed with a
Power Verse, determined not to leave Nantucket until I
had taken a step toward solving a serious problem which
had been emerging slowly over the years in my working
relationship with Tib.

"I want to apply Mark 4:22 to my problem, Lord," I
said: " 'For there is nothing hid, which shall not be manifested; neither was any thing kept secret, but that it
should come abroad.' Will You help me make manifest
the things which are hurting us?"

The problem had come into focus one day months
earlier when I went into Tib's office to sharpen a pencil.
It should have been a moment for a pleasant visit. Sun
poured onto her desk, leaving a pattern of colored light
from the stained glass design she had hung in her window. The cat was curled up next to her. Papers were
strewn about—always a good sign with Tib: the messier
her desk, the better she is working.

The manuscript under her pen was the last draft I had done on *The Hiding Place*. Tib was concentrating and paid no attention as I stuck my pencil into the sharpener and began to grind away. She was so intent that she never looked up while I ground that poor pencil to a stub. My eyes followed the intricate crossed-out lines and rewritten portions of my draft. She was changing everything!

I said not a word, but as I left the room I knew that we were headed for trouble.

Later, while Tib, binoculars in hand, was off on her daily birdwalk, I went back to her office and looked at the manuscript more closely. She had rewritten heavily, not only on that page but on previous pages too. Of course she was supposed to be rewriting. My job on this manuscript was to tell the story, give the narrative a forward thrust. Tib was to take this draft of mine and work on characterization, emotional development and immediacy. My work usually came first in time sequence. Although it was a draft, it wasn't a rough draft. Long ago I discovered that it was important for me to turn over to Tib the very best work I was capable of. This meant doing two to four rewrites, however many it took before I began to spin wheels.

It had been a successful partnership in many ways. But over the past few years some of the flaws in this plan began to show up.

Our problem began in this way: For years books and magazine articles we worked on were edited without our names appearing on them; so the problem of identity never came up. The first book on which our names appeared was *The Cross and The Switchblade*, with David Wilkerson, which Tib and I wrote and signed together. Our second signed book was *They Speak With Other Tongues*. That project too started off as a joint by-line effort: both our names would be on it. It was to be an

objective, somewhat distant, reporters' view of the pente-
costal movement.

And when the manuscript was just about finished, the
unthinkable happened. I received the Baptism in the Holy
Spirit myself. Our judicious objective viewpoint was gone!
We both felt there was nothing to do but toss away the
first version and start again. Now, instead of a report we
had a personal narrative. We tried to tell the story in the
first person plural, but it didn't work, the search and the
experience had to be told from the viewpoint of one person.

"And that person is you, John," Tib said. "I haven't had
this experience yet, you have. You should tell the story."
I agreed, too readily, as it turned out, and we wrote the
story that way. In our own home we thought of the book
as "ours," but that's not what people reading the story
thought. The book had my name on it, so naturally it was
John's. Tib assured me she had no problem with that.

The real problem followed when our other books also
became "John's."

Once, I actually witnessed for myself the phenomenon
Tib had to live with. We were at a conference together.
I watched an intelligent-looking, well-groomed lady come
up, carrying in her hand a copy of one of our books with
"John and Elizabeth Sherrill" plainly printed on the
jacket. The woman wrung Tib's hand. "This book of your
husband's has meant so much to me!" she said. Tib, better
at acting than I, exchanged a look with me then flashed
a convincing smile of appreciation at the woman.

For years we knew that there was a terrible tension
here. An unhappiness was building. In moments of high
communication Tib would tell me what it was like to
feel like a pane of window glass. "A smudged one, too,
because I feel so guilty about reacting this way."

"I don't know why it should be starting to bother me

now," she said to me one day as we drove in to a *Guideposts* meeting, "when I've worked anonymously for so many years. I've loved the privacy of not having my name on things. I think it's having become the-wife-of so much of the time that's getting to me. People need to be valued as *themselves*."

In the meanwhile, poison was setting in for me too. Long ago, in our own circle of writing friends, Tib's unique ability had become apparent. At the magazine we always turned to her when there was need for an especially sensitive story. Each month *Guideposts* surveyed a sampling of readers for reactions to stories: the most popular articles were those Tib had written or edited. Rising slowly to the threshold of consciousness was the fear that Tib was a better writer than I was. Like her, I knew that I *shouldn't* react this way. But in fact I am a very, very competitive person, and my own wife was emerging as a threat.

The relationship between us reminded me of a scene that once took place in the viewfinder of my camera. We were living in Uganda, and had just enrolled Scott, Donn and Liz in school. This was their first day, and each child was dressed in his school uniform, the boys in gray shorts and white shirts, Liz in a green and white checked dress and gray bowler hat. Each child also carried a yellow plastic bottle into which Tib had poured that regulation drink of all British school systems, a ghastly sweet liquid called Squash.

"I've got to get a picture of this scene," I said to Tib. "You line them up while I get the camera."

When I came back, the children were standing in a stair-step position, against the wall. I adjusted my lens openings, then raised the camera just in time to catch a drama in the viewfinder. Donn, three years younger than Scott, was on his tiptoes. In the camera he looked almost as tall as Scott. And then as I watched, Scott caught on. His face turned into a portrait of rage. He seized his younger brother by the shoulders. Through clenched teeth I heard him hiss, "You get down and you *stay* down."

I told that story once to a friend of ours, Virginia Lively, when I was trying to get at the root of my problem with Tib. Virginia has a gift from God in the area of healing. She listened, then laughed in her rolling, easy way.

"Competition does start early, John," she said. "It also dies late. Do you have a younger sister? I thought so. Maybe your competitiveness is still living inside you, only you have transferred it to another close, younger female, who is Tib."

This made a lot of sense, especially in light of the way *The Hiding Place* came into our lives. Tib met Corrie ten Boom while on a trip to Germany. It was love from the start. Tib came back flushed with excitement.

"I don't know whether I've done something wonderful or awful," she said as I drove her back from Kennedy Airport. "I've signed us up for a book."

I guess my face did show a certain blanched quality. So far, in the division of labor in our partnership, I had been the one to sign up the books. When Tib went on to outline the plot of Corrie's story to me, I was appalled. A middle-aged Dutch shopkeeper who was involved with the resistance movement in World War II? The story happened so long ago and so far away! Who would be interested in such a thing?

We should have decided then and there to let this be the first book Tib signed by herself. She suggested that, she says, although to this day I don't remember it. Was I, deep in my unconscious, telling her to get down and stay down?

In any event, I plunged ahead, blocked out the story,

wrote scenes, developed the narrative thrust. For some reason though, I was reluctant to turn the story over to Tib. Instead of doing two or three drafts I did five. Over and over the story I went, determined, I suppose, to have it so good that Tib would say, "Well, there's really nothing for me to do."

Then came the day when the last page of my work came back from the typist. In a little ceremony I handed it over to Tib.

"Please be with Tib now, Lord, as she takes this manuscript and adds, subtracts, highlights, brings to it her special genius."

What a hypocritical prayer that was!

As the weeks passed and Tib did add her special genius, I began to make more and more frequent trips into her office to sharpen pencils.

Finally my anger came out all at once. Very often we get our best talking done in the car, and so it was this time. We were driving to Washington. We got no further than the oil refineries of New Jersey before I brought up with Tib how I really felt about the way the manuscript was being changed.

It wasn't a polite exposition. My feelings spewed out of me. Tib listened in silence as I accused her of destroying not only my work but me.

What were we going to do? We both realized that we had hit a deep-rooted personal issue. But in the meanwhile there was a book at stake. Corrie, then in her seventies, was eager for her book to come out as fast as possible. We had a realistic time factor to consider. We couldn't just shelve the project. So by the time we reached the Delaware Memorial Bridge, we had decided on a practical strategy. We would ask our long-time friend, Arthur Gordon, then a Roving Editor for the *Reader's Digest*, to look at our two versions, side by side.

It was an awkward position to ask any friend to step into. Anyone with less empathy for the plight of writers would simply have refused. But Arthur heard our hurt and opened himself up to a lot of work and possible misunderstanding. I will never forget the day we met, two weeks later, in the penthouse of the Yale Club in New York, to which Arthur belongs, opposite Grand Central Station. We sat before a low table, in chairs that were too low for comfort, sampled peanuts from the bowl in front of us, and skirted the subject. Finally Arthur put our two manuscripts on the coffee table in front of him.

"There's no doubt that this is publishable," Arthur said, patting the version I had written. "It probably would do all right, too."

Then he put his hand on Tib's version. "But *this* now . . ." his eyes brightened, ". . . this work sings."

So, sitting now in the living room of Frank and Claire's house on Nantucket, I remembered how I had struggled out of my too-low chair at the Yale Club and walked around the room trying to handle my feelings. I put on my best good-sport manner. I told Tib she should feel free to do a complete rewrite on the manuscript without worrying about my feelings.

With my will I meant that. But as the weeks passed I began to realize that my emotions and my will were unrelated creatures. I couldn't fool Tib. Soon tension was building again. Our physical life together suffered. My work came to a stop. Even magazine articles, which I usually handled without trouble, became torture.

All right, I said to myself there in the Coffins' living room, where does this leave me? How should I face this problem? For one thing, it was clearly in the realm of work. We had "important" work to do, and for years we had let ourselves be persuaded that results came first. No

matter what the cost in personal growth, no matter how
snarled up our feelings were getting, results were what
mattered.

"All right, Lord," I said. "Every problem offers a choice.
I can move one step closer to You, or I can move one step
away from You. I choose to move toward You. Please,
before I leave this island, show me Yourself in this problem."

I asked God to show me Himself. He did, but not before
He showed me myself, and he did it through a common-
place kitchen appliance.

To this day I marvel at what happened there in the
Coffins' kitchen. Claire has a new appliance, a compactor,
which compresses table scraps, wastepaper, even glass
and tin cans into a small package which can then be dis-
posed of. It is a useful device, especially out in the country where trash pickup is infrequent. Since the first hours
of my visit here, six days ago, the machine had slowly
been filling up.

Then one morning I looked into the can of coffee and
realized that I was almost out. Now, the one thing which
can stop me at my work is to run out of coffee. So I decided to drive into Nantucket Center to do some shopping.

But the car key wasn't on the marble front hall table
where I was sure I had left it.

I looked in the bedroom, checked every jacket, emptied
my pants pockets. Nothing. Had I left it in the car? No.
Had I remembered to bring a spare key? Or was our
extra key in the glove compartment? No.

By now I was worried. It would take days for Tib to
mail a duplicate. I looked for another half hour then got
around, at last, to asking for help. "Lord," I said, "would
You please tell me where that key is?" It was a simple
prayer and I had hardly finished it before my eyes fell on
the compactor.

I opened the machine, bent over and looked inside. No key, of course. What a ridiculous idea! How could a car key fall into a trash compactor? How in fact could the key be in the kitchen at all since there was never any reason to bring it here. I lifted a lettuce leaf, laughing at myself. It was not exactly a pleasant task to go squishing around in crushed kitchen goo, but I picked up that lettuce leaf and looked. No key.

Of course, there wasn't! I turned away, intending to stop this search right there. But just then an incredible idea sprung to mind.

"Keep searching and you will find the key to your car and also the key to your problem."

I shook my head! What an odd thought. Yet I couldn't lose the feeling that the idea had come to me from God. So, despite all logic, I spread newspaper on the floor, rolled my sleeves up to the elbows, and with a sigh reached into that compactor.

Soon I had to start digging. What a mess. The deeper I got the more distasteful the waste became. Trash compacted on top of trash. Just like my problem with work, Lord?

Surely I wasn't supposed to take the parallel literally. Or was I?

I lifted out a smashed plastic tray from a carton of tomatoes. There goes the argument I had with Tib last week over final changes she was making in *The Hiding Place*. I removed a flattened wad of paper toweling. There goes the moment I had appropriated some of the applause that belonged to Tib.

Still I dug. There, as a crumpled aluminum tray from a TV dinner, go my anxieties about failure. Why did failure make me so uneasy? "You had to achieve in order to win love!" the Spirit whispered to me. "That is a lie you are uncovering. Keep digging. You are almost there."

One more layer of guck. I recognized the chicken dinner I had on my first night on the island six days ago. Now I was at the very bottom. It was runny, smelly, unpleasant work. I had long ago given up on the key. There was no way it could be under six days worth of refuse because I had used the car often since arriving, so even if by some freak chance the key *had* fallen into the compactor it couldn't be way down here. Why, then, was I continuing to dig? And why dig into the muck of my own past? Was it because, by the very process of bringing things to light,I was taking away their ability to damage?

I leaned back, wiped my hands dry and remembered our most recent visit with Jamie Buckingham, who had come to New York to attend an editorial meeting at *Guideposts.* The visit came shortly after I began to have trouble with work. Each morning I'd sit down to those menacing rows of keys, each evening I'd get up with those keys largely unused.

That night after the meeting Tib and I drove Jamie to his hotel. In the car we told him about our battle over *The Hiding Place,* and about how I hadn't been able to work since Arthur's verdict on the two manuscripts. As we drew up in front of Jamie's hotel and parked, Jamie asked me,

"What would happen if Tib wrote a book and signed it and you wrote a book and signed it and Tib's sold better?"

The answer I gave was intended to be flip. "It would kill me," I said.

Silence from Jamie and Tib.

"And that," said Jamie at last, "is what Tib knows. For years she's known."

"Oh come on now, you guys. I'm joking."

"What you really want," said Jamie, ignoring my protest, "is to be *better* than Tib. Not equal to, but *better.*"

Again there was silence. Truth had been spoken and there wasn't much else to say.

"Why are you reminding me of that, Lord?" I asked. Apparently, in order to feel worthwhile I had to earn love by feeling *better* than other people? What a devastating insight. The drive to excel, Virginia Lively suspected, dated back to childhood when I felt that to survive I had to be better than my sister. Taller, wiser, smarter, older. I still had the compulsion. I had to be bett*er* than Tib at writing. High*er* than someone else. I had to work hard*er* than other people. Was there no end to the Er-thans? "The Er-thans, Lord, are my undoing. They are the bottom of the soggy mass of emotions and just about as unappealing as this soup in the bottom of the compactor."

Fascinated by the analogy, I stirred the muck now with a knife. And while I was stirring in the last of the unpleasant sludge, there at the ultimate bottom of the compactor, all alone except for the top of one tin can, shone the bright, beautiful car key.

I reached in and took it out and put it respectfully onto a paper towel. Unbelieving, I sat down. I picked up the key and dried it off. I held it for a moment to the sun that flooded Frank and Claire's kitchen. I tossed it in the air. I turned it around, admiringly.

It was an utterly silent moment there in that isolated hilltop in the Nantucket springtime. I could hear no sound at all, not even the faint whir of motors that usually run offstage in any modern house.

I just sat there in the kitchen, holding the key in the palm of my hand, realizing that I was taking part in an unusual, acted-out conversation with God. It was a living parable. The automobile key had been in the garbage all along, and in some mysterious way I knew it. The key to my problems with Tib—the Er-than Syndrome—had

been in the garbage of my mind all along and in some
mystic way I knew that too.

I had come to the island with Mark 4:22 to speak into
the work problem I was facing. "For there is nothing hid,
which shall not be manifested; neither was any thing
kept secret, but that it should come abroad." That word
had been used to bring secrets to light but now I needed
another Power Verse which would help me drive away
th "Er-thans" whenever they appeared.

I got out my Bible and opened it on the kitchen table.
I turned to Luke 4 and re-read the account of Jesus'
second problem-temptation.

> And the devil, taking him up into an high mountain,
> shewed unto him all the kingdoms of the world in a mo-
> ment of time.
> And the devil said unto him, All this power will I give
> thee, and the glory of them: for that is delivered unto me;
> and to whomsoever I will I give it.
> If thou therefore wilt worship me, all shall be thine.
>
> Luke 4:5–7 KJV

As I read, the three words *kingdom* and *power* and
glory seemed to take on special importance. All three were
claimed by Satan as his domain. Yet even that could be
Satan's lie. Because there was another verse, the doxology
at the end of the Lord's own prayer, that claimed all three
for God: "For thine is the kingdom, and the power, and
the glory" (Matthew 6:13 KJV).

That then would be my Arsenal Verse. The glory and
the power of achieving did not belong to me. Any time I
claimed them, I would be stepping out of the Kingdom,
and into Satan's realm of lies.

Three years have passed since that experience with the

compactor in Frank and Claire's home in Nantucket. The
living parable remains as vivid in my memory as if it had
happened yesterday.

How much has changed? The most important shift has
come in my relationship with Tib. It is better across the
board. We still have our lively disagreements—I'd worry
if we didn't—but they are on specific issues and once
finished they are out of the way. Our family life has
never been so good. Our physical life has never been
better.

And our work?

We may one day start writing together again, using
different ground rules. But meanwhile, we decided that
we ought to work independently. *The Hiding Place* was
finished. Tib began thinking about a book she'd like to
write alone. I reminded myself of the "thanksgiving"
book I had determined to do, after my cancer scare in
England where all royalties would belong to God.

What better subject for my first solo effort than these
very discoveries I was making with the Bible?

And what better way to act on my new Arsenal Verse
than to turn any profits over to Him? *"Thine* is the
kingdom and the power and the glory!" So often the
little kingdoms we carve out for ourselves are based,
simply and bluntly, on money. "Money is power."
"Money is safety." To one afflicted with the Er-than
Syndrome, such slogans seemed all too believable.

By writing about the release I was finding in the Bible—and by accepting no money from the project—I
could fling one of Satan's lies back in his face.

That same week, even before I left Nantucket, I began
making notes for this book.

12.

ⁿↄↄↄↄↄↄↄↄↄↄↄↄↄↄↄↄↄↄↄↄↄↄↄↄↄↄↄ

Red Herring No. 3:
The Spiritual Attack

*THE MOST SUBTLE of Satan's onslaughts in the Judean
wilderness, he saved for last: the attack through the word
of God itself.*

> And he took him to Jerusalem, and set him on the pin-
> nacle of the temple, and said to him, "If you are the Son
> of God, throw yourself down from here; for it is written,
>   'He will give his angels charge of you, to guard you,'
> and
>   'On their hands they will bear you up,
>   lest you strike your foot against a stone.'"
> And Jesus answered him, "It is said, 'You shall not tempt
> the Lord your God.'"
>
> Luke 4:9–12 RSV

I stood looking at myself in the bathroom mirror. Red
lines wandered through my eyes. I had a heavy, bogged-
down feeling that I knew would interfere with the rest of
my day.

It was no mystery what the trouble was. Simple over-
indulgence. Years ago we started a system in our family

whereby first one, then the other of us would fix supper. When the boys were younger, their contribution was usually hamburgers or hotdogs. With Liz it might be hamburgers too, but the table would be set with her great-grandmother's china, candles, and from only-Liz-knew-where, a centerpiece.

Last night had been my turn. I started drinking early, while making the bouillabaisse. By the time dinner was ready I had made a major assault on the bottle of Bern-kastler.

Then there was wine with the meal too. Then wine with an hour in front of television. I chose Kojak rather than public television because there would be plenty of ad breaks, opportunities to slip out to the kitchen where I kept my supply of jug wine.

So that's why I stood in front of the mirror now, staring at my puffy eyes. And this wasn't before my conversion, it was fifteen years afterwards. Something was happening that I did not like at all.

Yet the use of wine, I reminded myself often, was Scriptural. The psalmist spoke of God's giving us "wine that maketh glad the heart of man . . ." (Psalm 104:15 KJV). Paul told Timothy to ". . . use a little wine for thy stomach's sake . . ." (1 Timothy 5:23 KJV). Wine was the common table drink of Palestine. Jesus drank wine and He created it at the first miracle He ever performed.

Oh, I'd often heard the argument—both in Kentucky where I grew up and later in other parts of the country—that the wine of the Bible was unfermented. But this seemed out of kilter with life in the Near East. It was certainly out of keeping with the accepted ways of many twentieth-century European Christians.

Years before, Tib and I were visiting a friend in her seaside home in Georgia. Betty came from a missionary family where she had been exposed to the tradition that wine in the Bible was grape juice. But just before our visit Betty had had to take a second look at that understanding after returning from a trip to Europe. One night she had been invited to dine with a dedicated Swiss Christian family. At the table was a devout, grandmotherly lady who reminded Betty of sweet elderly ladies she had known both in the U.S. and on the mission field. When Betty asked for water with her meal, however, the similarity collapsed. This dear lady was *shocked*. Water!? And she expressed her shock with many of the same phrases Betty had heard applied to wine. A Christian drank *water* instead of wine?! Water wasn't good for the system. Wine was healthier, and more Scriptural too!

Here, for the first time in Betty's experience, in a familiar Bible-centered setting, wine was accepted as a sanctified part of normal living. Real wine, not an unfermented beverage.

And what about the Bible? When Betty returned to Georgia she took time to go through the Bible, looking up every reference to wine. "When I was finished," Betty told us, "it was clear to me that whatever else you can say about Bible wine, it isn't grape juice."

I was certain of this too. Still, something was nagging at me, saying that in my case it was not all right to drink wine. Efforts at moderation failed. One drink with meals? Not for me: once I started, I always ended up having more, often secretly, out in the kitchen. Occasionally I would take a bootstrap stand, throw away all our wine and stop drinking altogether. Our friends were confused. Whenever we were invited for dinner the first question was, "John, are you on or off?"

Tib was thoroughly aware of my struggle so, although she enjoyed wine greatly, whenever I stopped she would stop too. I remember once when she agreed to the brave stand of giving away our stemware. We made this gesture just before taking a trip to Europe. Tib and I first met each other aboard a ship and we are still ocean liner buffs; if possible, when our work takes us to Europe, we go by ship. We were going by sea now. Friends brought champagne to the sailing party on the QE2. With self-conscious willpower, I poured glasses of bubbly for others, while I drank ginger ale and Tib drank Perrier water.

That effort lasted exactly two hours longer. We had just settled down in the dining room when the wine steward came by. We knew MacNeil from previous trips. His face lit up at the sight of such good customers. Fingering the great brass key which hung around his neck, MacNeil leaned over our table and placed the plush carte in front of me.

"What will you be eating tonight?" It was his way of asking what wine we wanted.

For a brief moment I battled. What about our forever-decision? What about the sacrifice of Tib's stemware? And all that ginger ale still cloying in my mouth!

But then, this did seem like a more than special occasion. I leaned toward Tib. "Maybe just for the trip?"

"You'll have to decide, honey."

And it was all over. I looked up at MacNeil and told him we'd start with a little light Mosel. Within one day, my drinking pattern was back to its full-fledged over-indulgence.

The change began on a trip to California.

Air travel has always been my nemesis. Those long hours in the airport! The chrome chairs, the endless, clattering corridors, the airline meals which our daughter-in-law Meg calls "plastic food units." It made time go faster to get aboard in a wineglow rather than to suffer the various indignities with my faculties in merciless focus. As usual I arrived at the airport with enough time to assure a meal at the Skyview Restaurant where I ordered lightly from the menu and heavily from the wine list.

When I got to the coast that evening I checked in at our favorite motel in the area, the Casa Malibu, an old fashioned bougainvillaea-draped place right on the Pacific. I unpacked, prepared to follow my usual pattern of taking a quick trip down to the Sea Lion Restaurant for a winy fish dinner.

But what was happening? Why wasn't I getting ready? The sun was about to set. It would be a perfect time to sit at a window table looking over the rocky beach.

Still I did not go. Instead, I opened the sliding glass doors of my room and went out onto the motel deck, just feet away from the ocean. I sat down in one of the Casa Malibu's bent-bamboo chairs and put my feet up on the weathered, two-by-four railing.

Gently, gently a voice began speaking inside of me. I thought I recognized it as the still voice of the Lord. He was saying, "What area do you think your problem with alcohol is in? Is it physical?"

Physical? I could certainly feel the desire pulling at me right there, sitting on the porch. Yes, that was it, I had a physical addiction.

"Are you sure?"

Well, maybe there was more to it.

"How about your work . . . is this a work problem?"

It was certainly that. Remember that interview last month when I asked questions through a morning-after haze? Yes, this was a work problem.

"Are you sure?"

Thoroughly bewildered, I waited but heard nothing more. So I got up, stepped back through the glass doors and found my Bible. There was only one temptation-area left. I re-read how Satan challenged Jesus to throw Himself from a pinnacle of the temple; He would be safe because He had special divine protection. Jesus answered, "It is said, 'You shall not tempt the Lord your God'" (Luke 4:12 RSV).

I did not see the parallel. What did the temptation to jump from a pinnacle have to do with drinking? I could not reach a conclusion that night, but neither did I go to the Sea Lion.

I did go the next evening, however, with my writer friend Bob Owen. We sat now at the very window booth which I had intended to occupy last evening, with waves crashing on the rocks below. A diver, looking for the world like Neptune, came out of the sea dressed in a wet suit and carrying a three-pronged spear. A waitress wearing white space shoes bent over us.

"What will you have to drink?"

Bob said, "Nothing thanks," and I found myself saying I didn't want anything either. So the waitress put two outsized menus down before us and padded off. As soon as she was gone I spoke to Bob about my puzzlement.

"I've been trying to stop drinking, Bob. With very little success I might say. I keep falling back. Part of my problem is that wine is so Biblical."

Bob leaned back on the plastic seat and once again I had the experience of hearing the clarion voice of God in the casual remark of a friend. I'm sure Bob did not know he was speaking for God, but that's typical of this kind of prophecy. He said quietly, "I understand. You're abusing your Scriptural privilege."

The words crashed through my mind. Bob turned his attention to the tabloid-sized menu, but my mind clutched at what he had just said. Abuse of Scriptural privilege! Of course. That's why this was a *spiritual* problem. That's why the Lord had led me last night to the third of Jesus' temptations, where Satan threw a spiritual decision at

Jesus. He reminded Jesus quite accurately, that He had a privileged position. Angels would care for Him so completely that He would not even stub His toe. He *could* in fact appear on the pinnacle of the temple, as ancient tradition foretold the Christ would do, then demonstrate His Messiahship by a spectacular leap, walking away unscathed before the adoring throng. But Jesus knew that this wasn't at all the Father's route for Him. Jesus had a far harder, more agonizing road to follow. To duck the agony would not please the Father. And, as always, Jesus chose the route that left Him in the Father's company.

The waitress was back again, pencil poised. Bob ordered while I made a quick, finger-stabbing decision from the menu. We went on to talk about other things and never did get back to the subject so much on my mind.

But later that evening, sitting again in the moonlight on the raw-wood deck of the motel, I compared my temptation with Jesus'. I had the full Scriptural privilege of drinking wine. But in my case to use that privilege would be to abuse it. I had taken wine past the point of joy, health and gladness of heart. To expect God to protect me, keep me safe physically, emotionally and spiritually while continuing to abuse wine would be to deliberately challenge Him.

That night I got around at last to doing what Jesus did. He used a verse of Scripture against Satan's temptation, and I would do the same. I asked the Father to give me the defensive tool that I could use forever in my problem-temptation.

And He did, by bringing to mind a verse I had heard all my life. That is I *thought* I had heard it. The portion I knew said, "Resist the devil, and he will flee from you" (James 4:7 KJV).

But for some reason I had never seen this quotation in its entirety. For when I went inside and looked up the reference I found that the complete verse is, "Submit yourselves therefore to God. Resist the devil and he will flee from you." That's not two verses, it's one. One thought: Submit first, then you can resist.

I must strike an attitude of submittedness to the Lord on this issue of alcohol. It would have to be a permanent way of life. I had goofed. I had abused a Scriptural privilege. The result was a near disaster. My job was no longer to try to change myself but to put abstinence in His keeping. Then in an attitude of yieldedness I could resist Satan by availing myself of *God's* power as it flowed dynamically through my Arsenal Verse.

I have not had a drink since that day. Satan has tried to undermine my freedom by hurling counterfeit motive-verses at me. When Satan tires of this, he whispers that my new approach is no different from other forever-decisions. But Satan is lying. This time *is* different because I am no longer depending on myself. I am free because God makes me free, not because I am strong or have risen above my problem.

I still need, quite regularly, to call on my Power Verse. But every time I do, the results are the same: the temptation itself disappears and I move one small step closer to God.

13.

The Unfolding Master Plan

I HAD BEGUN to see, over the past months, that Jesus in the wilderness was revealing a Master Plan for handling problems.

I
Before the Battle

The first step in that plan required me to do some work *before* problems emerged. I should have certain tools and attitudes at the ready.

1) I would have at least 100 Arsenal Verses stored and ready to use on the instant.

2) I would not be dismayed at the presence of problems in my life, remembering that the Spirit Himself led Jesus, and He also leads me, into the wilderness.

3) I will be confident that I can distinguish Satan's voice from God's in the upcoming problems.

Satan will try to lead me away from my desire to focus on God. I can identify Satan's presence by the Holy Spirit's gift of the Discerning of Spirits

(1 Corinthians 12:10). My discernment will be
confirmed if I observe some distinctive satanic
traits. For the devil will always try to leave me:
* with my eyes turned toward the problem
  rather than toward God
* grasping at thoughts that will prove my own
  "superiority"
* feeling judgmental and self-righteous
* stirred up, angry
* unyielded, with myself in control
* abusing privileges of power or freedom
* trying to go around a problem, not through it.

II
In the heat of Battle

During the encounter itself I will both swiftly and
with simplicity put into practice the Three Only's of
Jesus:

1) There is *only one problem*, which is to stay in God's
   presence.
2) There is *only one hope*. If I want to face my problem the way Jesus did I can hope in God's strength
   alone, not in my own cleverness, or in any other ally.
3) There is *only one weapon* which I can draw upon if
   I follow Jesus' example, and that is the correct use
   of Power Verses which the Father highlights on a
   page of Scripture or brings to my mind from my
   arsenal of verses.

   I can be confident that I have heard God's choice
   of Scripture because God's verse for me for this
   situation leaves me:
   * looking toward Him and not toward the prob-
     lem
   * finding Him in the midst of the problem

* filled with a confidence that has absolutely
  nothing to do with the externals of the situation
* waiting expectantly to see what He will do
* at peace, even in these most difficult circumstances.

III
After the Battle

After countering Satan's temptations I will watch to
see how God will put me to work.

How well I remember the day I first began to suspect
that there *was* an "after" stage in the Master Plan. The
possibility began to emerge immediately following my
first trip without alcohol.

"Lord, I can't handle this alone," I reminded myself on
the morning of the flight. "It's not my strength but Your
word that will be effective today." I repeated aloud the
James 4:7 verse which God had given me for battle,
"Submit yourselves therefore to God. Resist the devil and
he will flee from you."

At the airport there was the usual wait between
check-in and boarding the plane for Charlotte. But with
the help of this verse I spent my time not having wine
at the bar but working on my speech.

The verse was alive in my mind when the stewardess
came by a few minutes after take-off for drink orders.
"I'll have a Bloody Mary mix, please. Just the mix."

She smiled at me. "We call that a Bloody Shame," she
said.

Later there was the lonely evening in the hotel. Here
too, I ate my dinner and went up to the room without
so much as a glass of California chablis.

That was what I remembered about the trip to Charlotte. With the help of the power inherent in a verse of

Scripture, spoken into a situation, an old temptation had been successfully withstood.

But apparently something else also took place on that trip. I remember meeting Martin after the conference. I recall that he was in his mid-fifties, lean to the point of gauntness, wore his hair in a then-unstylish crew cut. Martin had just seen his family business go into receivership and he needed someone—not from the Charlotte area—to talk to. For an hour we sat on a stone bench in the garden of the conference center and just visited. While Martin told me about his feelings I prayed silently. Then I made one or two observations. That was it.

And yet, after I returned to New York, Martin wrote not just once but three times to say how much that hour in the garden meant to him. Those minutes, he said, had changed his life.

How could that possibly be!

I had not felt that my comments were especially wise or penetrating. Obviously, the Holy Spirit had used me as a vehicle to reach Martin. Could it be that I had been usable in this case because, for once, I had encountered a problem in my own life *without* stepping outside of the Spirit?

Several weeks later, still another verse of Scripture helped me win a battle against an ailment common to so many men and women—the sexual fantasy. Much current literature does not consider this a problem at all, but a pleasant escape from loneliness or frustration or rejection. With me it began early in my marriage as a mild form of escapism, tied to loneliness—or more to the point, aloneness.

It didn't matter whether Tib went away from me, or I from her; it didn't matter whether we were apart for business or family reasons. My response was usually the same: my thought patterns went on a binge.

For a while it was all in my mind. Then the time came when I began to drift over to magazine stands and thumb through pornographic literature. As time passed, I started to buy these magazines. Then if I were lonesome in a distant city some strange sense told me where the X-rated movies were. This never happened except when I was separated from Tib.

I reacted to this pattern in two ways. I could imagine one set of friends saying, "I don't understand your worry. You're too goody-goody. What are you, some kind of monk?" Or I could imagine another set of friends saying, "You are a Christian now and supposedly born again to new and victorious life. When are you going to grow up?"

The trouble was that after listening to these two imaginary conversations, which doubtless reflected two sides of my own personality, I knew without doubt which was the real me. Those secret adventures were a most serious matter *for me* for two reasons. There was always the possibility that thoughts would become deeds; this was Satan's goal. Secondly, exposure to sex material always got directly in the way of my ability to focus on God.

So it was clear to me that I should change. And that's precisely where the trouble came, because try as I might, my will power did not help me. I always went right ahead with the same old reaction every time Tib and I were separated; and later I always reacted to these escapes in the same way too, determining to mend my ways. But when next time rolled around I went through the same response.

I took the issue to a psychiatrist friend. He had a name for it. "We call your compulsion a 'separation anxiety syndrome,'" the doctor said. "If it's any comfort, and it probably isn't, you've got lots of company."

The doctor was right. It wasn't much comfort thinking

of the large number of people who fought this same battle. Several weeks later as Tib was getting ready for a trip, I became numb with anxiety. For when she was gone, if I followed my usual pattern, I knew exactly what I would do.

Still . . .

Then the thought came—have you tried the Bible? I had not been dynamic in putting the Bible to work against this compulsion. The pattern was too old. What if it failed! Besides, the Bible would probably try to correct me and I already *knew* how I should be acting.

But now, as Tib went up to pack, I remembered that I hadn't even tried to read my Bible that morning. We still had an hour before time to leave for the airport. So reluctantly I went down to my office, found the appointed selection and read Joshua's challenge to the people of Israel, who were being tempted to follow other gods. My pulse quickened. I really didn't want to hear another sermon.

Then, all of a sudden, there it was. The now-familiar experience of a verse standing out from the page. But this time there was something different. It was as if God knew perfectly well that I needed a new approach to my difficulty. If I had been so thoroughly conditioned by defeat that I was beaten before I even started, something different was needed. And He gave it to me. For these were the eight words that illuminated themselves on the page, ". . . choose you this day whom ye will serve . . ." (Joshua 24:15 KJV).

I put the Bible down, for I knew I was at a watershed.

Make up your mind *now*, Joshua was saying to the people, whom you will serve. Here was a guideline for recurring and predictable problems. I shouldn't try to do battle at the *point* of temptation. With my old record I had preconditioned myself to fail. But suppose I reversed that and preconditioned myself to success by fighting the battle *now*, ahead of time, while I was still on solid ground, before I got into the quagmire.

"Lord, I do just what Joshua did," I said aloud, standing there in my office. "Not later, but now, *this day*, I choose to serve You and not feed this salacious interest."

Tib left. And sure enough, as predictable as a tide this compulsion rolled in. The drive engulfed me: come on, slip out to the nearest dealer. In the past my will power had not saved me from the irresistible undertow.

But not now. I just didn't yield.

Not because I had suddenly become stronger, but because I had set my course ahead of time. The application of my Power Verse occurred hours ago, not at the point of temptation. And that made all the difference.

The remarkable thing was that although I was still faced with the old compulsion, I was never really tempted. Every time the alluring ideas flicked at my emotions I reminded myself of the word from Joshua and discovered that the battle had already been won.

To this day whenever I face separation, I prepare ahead of time with God's Power Verse, confident that He will then fight my battle for me.

Perhaps this is what Jesus had in mind when He taught His disciples the model defensive prayer, "Lead us not into temptation, but deliver us from the evil one." Perhaps He meant that we should try to avoid confronting Satan at the point of our greatest weakness, but that we could ask the Father to provide our delivery ahead of time. Then when the struggle comes, victory is already there. . . .

Well, it happened that just after this first triumphant experience with an old temptation, a woman telephoned who was facing a crisis in her home. Her teen-age daughter had run away with a married man, and now wanted to come back home. The woman's husband threatened to throw the girl out bodily if she dared "so much as to open my door." Again, just as I had done with Martin a few weeks earlier, we talked, but I cannot remember saying anything that sounded to *me* like wisdom; although it is true that an odd boldness swept over me as we talked and prayed together. When I asked God to come to the rescue of this family I sensed His closeness.

Our phone visit was over. In due course Tib came back home and then one night the phone rang again. It was the woman with the crisis at home.

"You'd probably like to know," she said, "how our prayers were answered. Things are not only all right at home, they're better than they've ever been."

What was going on!

As I reviewed these two recent experiences, with Martin and this lady, it was clear to me that some uncustomary force was flowing through me, a formidable intercessory energy that went way beyond my own ability to help. Surely it was related to successful handling of problem-temptations. If Satan treats problems as red herrings, trying to get us to focus on our trials rather than on God . . . and if we say No to that temptation, then maybe afterwards we are always given a job to do.

Did this happen to Jesus?

I opened my Bible to see. I knew that He had gone into His temptation in the Spirit, and that He came out of the wilderness still in the Spirit, but it came as a surprise to me that this experience was *immediately* followed by the beginning of Jesus' ministry to people in need. He spelled out exactly what He would be doing:

> The Spirit of the Lord is upon me, because he hath anointed me to preach the gospel to the poor; he hath sent me to heal the brokenhearted, to preach deliverance to the captives, and recovering of sight to the blind, to set at liberty them that are bruised.
>
> Luke 4:18 KJV

There it was, all in one chapter. I turned to Matthew and Mark and they told the same story, making a direct linkage between being led into problems *by* God, taking an active step in the middle of the problem *toward* God, and then being put to work *for* God.

The pattern was too clear to miss. Handled correctly all our problems are going somewhere! They then immediately lead into work for others. We will be given a job to do. It is special work, prepared for us by the Lord ahead of time. "For we are his workmanship, created in Christ Jesus for good works, which God prepared beforehand, that we should walk in them" (Ephesians 2:10 RSV).

And often these good works which God has prepared for us are full of surprises and adventure which we could never plan for or anticipate.

14.

෨෨෨෨෨෨෨෨෨෨෨෨෨෨෨෨෨෨෨෨෨෨෨෨෨෨෨෨෨෨

Surprises and Adventure

I SUPPOSE, IF I were to search the globe I could not have found a more perfect job than I had at *Guideposts*.

I certainly would not have guessed this at first, though. I'll never forget Tib's father's comment, "What in the world can you see in that little sheet?"

At the time, we agreed. The little sheet was founded in 1945 by Dr. Norman Vincent Peale as a non-profit, interfaith newsletter designed for businessmen. Soon the newsletter evolved into a magazine intended not just for businessmen, but for their families too. Dr. Peale and a young editor, Len LeSourd, sought stories of people who found that their faith played an important role in practical everyday decisions.

In 1950, when the magazine had a circulation of just a few thousand, Tib and I arrived in New York, back from three years of free-lancing in Europe. Our first baby was due in October. I started looking for work just as the *New York Sun* merged with the *World Telegram*, throwing scores of trained men and women onto the streets looking for any kind of editorial work. Fall came. Scott was born October 2 and now there were three of us to feed. I remember arriving at one address in late November to answer an ad. A line of perhaps thirty men and women stood waiting in the trash-filled wind, hands in pockets, scarves covering their mouths and ears. We were all applying for the same writing job on a trade journal. I just walked away; I didn't even try.

Winter stretched on; December of 1950 became January of 1951. Tib's father talked me out of taking a job as an insurance salesman and encouraged me to keep looking in my chosen field of writing. To help out in the interim, he offered me part-time employment with his private detective agency, the Schindler Bureau of Investigation—a famous New York institution whose case files formed the base for many of Erle Stanley Gardner's yarns. The job forever dispelled any idea of glamour in shadow work. For one two-week stint I sat in a car watching the door of a Brooklyn warehouse. But the job did provide rent and food for Tib and Scott and me while, at every opportunity, I answered ads.

And then one day a small notice appeared in the *New York Times:* "Religious editor sought." The address of an agency was given. I decided to try. This in spite of the fact that I was neither an editor, nor was I religious. At least, I thought, there wouldn't be many applicants. And sure enough when I got to the address only two men stood on the sidewalk in front of the door. I got in line, my heart beating a little more rapidly, and began to wait.

Then came the shocker. For as the line moved and I stepped through the door, I saw that the two men were simply the tail end of a line that wound three flights up the stairwell. Once again I knew that it was hopeless.

But then an idea occurred to me. I'd often noticed that businessmen will desert the flesh and blood person in front of them and reach for a ringing telephone. What would happen if I *phoned* the employment agency!

I abandoned my place in the line (there were now two new men behind me), went around the corner to a Nedick's hamburger stand, dropped a nickel in the coin slot and in two minutes found myself talking with a lady in that office on the third floor.

"I can't get up to see you now . . ." I said. I didn't explain *why* I couldn't get up to see her now. ". . . but perhaps we could make an appointment for four?"

It worked. That afternoon I climbed the empty stairs and sat down for a leisurely visit with the agent. She made a series of notes and ended by handing me a pamphlet with the word "Guideposts" written across the top.

"Would you be free to meet these people tomorrow?"

Well, yes, I guessed I could arrange to be free . . .

At noon the next day I was sitting in a canary yellow office that had once been the telephone exchange for the Beekman Towers Hotel, talking with Len LeSourd. I thought the interview was going pretty well until Len dropped in, routinely, a request to see samples of my inspirational writing.

I thought fast. "Wouldn't it be better if I did an original piece for you?" I asked.

"Good idea," Len said, picking up several back copies of the magazine for me to study. "Let me see something in a week."

I spent days in our little apartment in Yonkers, New York, alternately admiring Scott who smiled at me from his wicker laundry basket and going over with Tib the concept and execution of an "inspirational" story, whatever in the world that meant. I wrote about the day early in World War II when I was called home from basic training so that my father could see me one last time before he went entirely blind. The story included a lightning-fast reference to my faith (which didn't bear any longer scrutiny than that), and I turned the story in.

"Mr. Sherrill? Would you hold the line please, Leonard LeSourd calling."

It was three days later. Three days of remembering changes I'd liked to have made in the script. But there was LeSourd's voice on the line telling me—incredibly— that everyone liked the article and wondered whether I could come into the city to be interviewed by Norman Vincent Peale.

Next day I sat in a taxicab driving pell mell between CBS and NBC. The famous Dr. Peale was on his way from one television interview to another, to discuss his then-current best seller *The Power of Positive Thinking.* The only free time in his day was during this one taxicab ride. It made me feel in the middle of big and important things. Dr. Peale asked what I most wanted out of life, gave me some advice about keeping my eye on quality, and then the cab was pulling up before NBC.

"Sorry we couldn't have more time together young man," Dr. Peale said. "This book of mine keeps me scurrying. You'll hear from Len."

I did, too. Things looked good. There was only one further hurdle. I had to pass muster with Executive Editor Grace Perkins Oursler, wife of the writer Fulton Oursler. Grace was a dry alcoholic, who guided the policies of the magazine from her sickbed in a suite at the Navarro Hotel overlooking Central Park. When I arrived, Grace was in the midst of writing a memo to the magazine. She showed it to me. Already the memo was four pages long. It had to do with "the *imperative* need for *standardizing* our punctuation at *Guideposts!!*" Grace didn't really interview me, she tried to give me her own excitement about this little pamphlet. "I can't tell you how important

Guideposts is," Grace said, punching a copy of the magazine on her bed. "Someday we'll have two—even three
hundred thousand circulation! You wait and see. Are you
Catholic?"

"No, Ma'am," I said remembering that Grace was a
fervent Catholic.

"Good. One like me is enough. As far as I'm concerned
you've got the job."

Thus began an immensely satisfying career at the magazine. Tib soon joined the staff. *Guideposts* offered us
security, challenge, support . . . and more, for in 1959
Tib and I both discovered personally what *Guideposts*
was all about. We became Christians. Our closest friends
were also our co-workers. Knowing that we both were
born with itchy feet *Guideposts* encouraged our love to
travel. The magazine sent us to Africa for a year, and
later to South America for a similar stint, to teach writing
to Christian leaders in newly literate countries. Meanwhile the magazine was thriving; by the late 1960's we
had two million paid subscribers.

Then with incredible swiftness Tib and I were weaned
away from the comfort, the security, the adventure and
the acceptance of our jobs at *Guideposts*.

I was awake. There had been no transition between
sleep and being fully, startlingly awake. Quietly, so as
not to disturb Tib, I propped my pillow against the head-
board of the bed and sat up. In the pre-dawn light I
could just make out the bureau in the corner of the room.
I couldn't understand it. Over there, against the wall . . .
what was that? Or was it inside my head? I stared more
intently. Just in front of my eyes, as if I were dreaming,
yet I knew I was awake, there appeared . . . a picture.

The picture was in black and white. It was of a group of people—Len LeSourd was there, and Len's wife, Catherine Marshall, Tib and I and some others I could not identify. We were all studying a pile of books spread out on a conference table. Beneath the picture there appeared to be an advertisement of some kind. The headline read "Adventures in Faith." A block of copy said that this group of people had worked together for years, writing and editing Christian articles. Now they had banded together to do the same with books. They would search the world for books that would have two criteria. They would be *interesting*. They would be *helpful*.

The vision was over. I could not get back to sleep so I went downstairs and made coffee.

I wished Tib would get up. I was excited but was also stunned, full of fear and misgivings. I knew nothing at all about business, still less about book publishing; what did all this mean? Surely I wasn't being asked at this step in my life to get into a new field of endeavor!

When Tib began to stir I took coffee up and told her about the vision and asked her what she thought of starting a publishing house. To my astonishment, Tib who knew, if possible, less about business than I, said, "Why not! It would be an adventure."

"That's for sure," I said.

On my next visit to New York I found two old friends in the office, Van Varner and Harold Hansen, who had started their own small public relations company and now had the magazine as a client. I asked them what they thought the chances were for a new publishing company that applied to books the writing principles we had learned at *Guideposts*. From experience both pointed out the pitfalls—the incredibly hard work, the loneliness, the very real financial risk. But through these cautionary notes came an overtone of excitement. To my amazement they did not question for a moment that I had actually been told to start a publishing company.

So I took the plunge, went into the boss' office and spoke to Len LeSourd. I told him about the vision and asked him if he and Catherine would consider joining us. As I talked, Len, who had been signing letters, put down his pen, swiveled his chair around and placed his fingertips together. When I finished he said he thought God might indeed have been speaking to us all in what I'd seen.

The next day Len called me at home with the news that he and Catherine were definitely interested. A heroine of Catherine's had always been Mary Roberts Rinehart not only as a writer but also because she helped found Farrar Rinehart Publishing Company.

"But . . ." said Len, and then came the words that were such a threat to me, "we couldn't join you now, of course. We couldn't publish books and work at *Guideposts* at the same time. That creates a problem for you too. You'll have to talk to the Peales, won't you." It wasn't a question, it was a statement.

I put down the phone slowly, drawing in a long, long breath. The Peales? I wasn't ready for that. Suppose I did have to leave *Guideposts*. It wasn't just the checks that came in every other week. Or the travel. Or meeting people we'd never have the chance to meet otherwise. The real problem with leaving *Guideposts* was leaving friends.

Couldn't I just say nothing? Wait until the company had a few books going?

When I told Tib about the dilemma at lunch that day I could tell she was alarmed too; she gouged away at her grapefruit until it was in shreds. It did sound risky, she said, to leave our jobs at this stage in our lives. Then she put down her spoon and added,

"But it isn't right to be sneaky either. You're experimenting with taking things to the Bible. Maybe there's a verse for you. One that will help you face this problem by facing God."

While Tib was still speaking, the beginning words of a verse came to mind, a verse that had played a role in an article I'd written recently: "Walk in the light . . ." I found it in First John:

> If we say that we have fellowship with him, and walk in darkness, we lie, and do not the truth: But if we walk in the light, as he is in the light, we have fellowship one with another . . .
>
> I John 1:6, 7 KJV

If we walked in the light we did not need to worry about losing fellowship!

I went straight to the phone and called the Peales. Sure enough, in the midst of Dr. Peale's still frantic schedule we found an evening.

Now Tib and I and Ruth and Norman were sitting in the comforting warmth of candlelight in a French restaurant near the Peales' home in Pawling, New York. Both Norman and Ruth looked better than I had seen them in years, fresh, slim, their faces full of color.

Over *moules* we talked about daring to step into the unknown. I told the Peales about my early morning vision, about the possibility of forming a new company and about the risks that seemed built into the idea. Both Norman and Ruth were intrigued and I wondered if their thoughts were going back to the days when they first caught the dream of founding a magazine.

"If only we didn't insist on security!" said Norman. "The unknown, that's where adventure lies. Would you like a year's leave of absence?" It was a perfect solution to our separation problems, but Norman raced on. He had something else he wanted to say. His next words were to affect the very shape of the company that was even then being born.

"If God is leading you into Christian books, I have a suggestion," Norman said. "You've heard me talk about the key to success in any undertaking. Six words. *Find a need and fill it.*

"And I'll tell you the need that I see. When I look at some of the Christian books coming across my desk, I'm appalled. Sloppy writing, sloppy editing, sloppy manufacturing. Aim for *quality*, John. Strive for it. Hold out for it even though it costs you time and money.

"Take a year off. Take the risk of living without a salary. Find adventure. And hold on to quality."

So we plunged ahead. We even had a Power Verse, given to us as an especial encouragement. "For we are his workmanship, created in Christ Jesus unto good works, which God hath before ordained that we should walk in them" (Ephesians 2:10 KJV). Our job was simply to walk the path He had planned for us.

Of course our infant company, which we called Chosen Books, had no titles. The most obvious first book was *The Hiding Place*. The manuscript was ready. It had been a battleground where we tried to grasp the principle of keeping our eye on God. Was that very book now ready to be put to use?

But *The Hiding Place* was already under contract at World Publishing Company. Perhaps we could buy it back? How much would World charge? Could we pay for the rights over an extended period, perhaps on a royalty basis?

But wait a minute. All this calculating went against the very Power Verse God had given us for our work. We

were created for ". . . good works, which God hath before ordained that we should walk in them." If our work
was already ordained then maneuvering was out of place.

I picked up the phone and called World's chief executive officer, Martin Levin, to ask for an appointment.

Tib and I were waiting, now, in the reception room of
the corporate headquarters of World Books. Pretty dra-
matic. Even the secretaries had secretaries. We were
passed up the line through rooms where the carpets got
deeper and the wood darker until at last we were ushered
into the magnificent offices of Martin Levin himself,
where the view over midtown Manhattan was spectacular.
Three chairs were waiting, placed familiarly around a
conference table where Mr. Levin stood with hand out-
stretched.

After we had settled down I reminded Mr. Levin
(World published scores of books each year) that we
were under contract with his company to write a book
with Corrie ten Boom.

To my surprise Mr. Levin remembered. "Interesting
theme," he said. "Spinster lady turns underground hero.
I think we'll do a good job with it."

I cleared my throat. "Well as a matter of fact that's
why we're here. We'd like to buy back the contract."

Mr. Levin didn't show any reaction at all. "What do
you want it for?" he asked.

"We want to go into publishing," I said quickly. "*The
Hiding Place* would be our first book." I fully expected
Mr. Levin to lean back and laugh. But instead he seemed
interested in the idea and asked for details.

"Publishing is a very tricky field, you know," Mr. Levin
said when I had explained our dream. "Especially today.
Prices are rocketing. Paper's scarcer. If you're small,

printers want their money up front. Salesmen need salaries
as well as commissions today. The after-tax return on
capital in this industry is a disaster; you can do better in
any savings bank."

I tried to look as though I had pondered all these
things at length. But then the idea came into my mind,
"Don't try to be anything you're not. Don't use strategy,
don't urge. Just walk." So I repeated my Arsenal Verse
to myself and mysteriously, without transition, Mr. Levin
changed the subject. I couldn't tell whether he was giving
himself time to think over what we were saying or
whether he was giving *us* time to think over all the logical
reasons why we shouldn't get into publishing. "Do you
know what the word 'dybbuk' means?" he asked.

I looked at Tib who used to curl up with a dictionary
at the age when I read comic books.

"Something like a poltergeist?" she asked.

Martin Levin picked up his telephone and punched
some buttons. From the conversation that followed it
dawned on me that Mr. Levin was calling *Cleveland*,
where the World Encyclopedia is published, just to learn
the meaning of a word. Mr. Levin put the phone down.
"You were right, Mrs. Sherrill. A dybbuk is a figure from
Jewish folklore, a free-floating spirit seeking a body to
live in."

Mr. Levin got up from his desk and stuck out his hand
to Tib. She rose to take it, and I rose too. He began
walking across the acre of pile, with us reluctantly following. Was the interview over? Was this the abrupt close-
out to our hopes?

"You're sure you want to take your title back?" he
said at the door.

Mr. Levin had asked the central question: were we
sure?

And I answered, not on the basis of logic, but because I still had fresh in mind that picture I had been given so unexpectedly, so completely unsought, yet so real, as if it were something that already existed.

"Yes, Mr. Levin. I am sure."

He nodded. "Then we certainly won't stand in your way." He walked us to the elevator bank. "Congratulations, on being our newest competitors."

The elevator doors opened. We stepped inside. Martin Levin smiled good-bye as the doors shut.

We looked at each other in amazement. We had just watched a Power Verse help us by putting aside all temptation to operate in our own cleverness. Within half an hour we had become a new publishing company with something more than just a name. We also had our first title. And we had a strange confidence too that *The Hiding Place* would now go on to be used by God in unusual ways.

So Chosen Books was launched. In 1974, Len, who had expected to be at *Guideposts* all his life, had a direct word from God that he was to resign and trust Him for the future. Some months later he and Catherine did join us as partners. It's not lip service to say we can't take credit for anything the little company achieves. The four of us are so ill-equipped to run any kind of business that the credit *has* to go to the Lord. What we do have is a Master Plan for handling the problems that arise daily in this scary, stretching business. Allow yourself to be led into problems *by* God; walk through your trials with your eyes *on* God; and expect to be put to work *by* God.

15.

~~~~~~

When Problems
Have No Answer. . .

IT WAS EARLY in the morning, Memorial Day, 1977. Tib and I were taking a few days off at a family cabin in upstate New York. The place was idyllic: a lake where no motorboats were allowed, miles of hilly paths, weather so cool we had a fire every morning, no telephone closer than the cabin next door.

Out of the corner of my eye I caught sight of our next-door neighbor now, coming up the steps.

"John?" the man called through the screen door. "I've just had a call from your sister. She wants you to phone her right away. Your mother has had a fall. She's in the Kentucky Baptist Hospital in Louisville."

A fall! Mother was going to be 79 next month. A fall at her age was not good news!

I followed my neighbor next door and within a few minutes was on the phone with my sister, Mary Durham, who lives in Washington, D.C.

"The news isn't good," Mary said. "Mother was all by herself at home. You know how independent she is . . ."

Yes, I knew how independent she was! Mother was planning, someday, when she got old, to sell her home and enter Westminster Terrace, a Presbyterian retirement residence nearby. But that wasn't for years and years.

"Apparently Mother tripped on a rug in her bedroom," Mary said.

Bit by bit the story came out. It was a horror tale. Mother had been planning to visit friends. They were to pick her up in the late morning. As Mother was getting ready she tripped, fell, broke her leg so badly she was unable even to crawl to the telephone. Mother heard her friend's car drive up the crunchy gravel driveway. She heard the doorbell ring. She called. And called. The friend didn't hear her. After a while the friend got back into her car and Mother heard the automobile once again crunch out of the driveway. Finally it occurred to Mother that she could roll to the telephone. In agony she worked her way to within reach of the telephone cord. She pulled. The instrument tumbled off the table and struck her head. But Mother managed to dial Margaret Durham, Mary's husband's mother, who was a close friend and neighbor.

Within an hour Mother was in the Kentucky Baptist Hospital. The femur was broken. An immediate operation was scheduled to put in a pin.

"Can she talk on the telephone?" I asked Mary.

"Yes. There's a phone next to her bed."

So I called Mother. She talked freely about the accident, repeating the story I had already heard.

Then, out of the blue, came the first hint of something far more serious, even, than a broken leg.

"There's one thing I don't understand, John . . ." Mother said.

"What's that, Mother?"

"I don't understand where the Egyptians fit into this whole equation."

The Egyptians? What Egyptians was she talking about. Before I had a chance to ask her, Mother had changed the subject, discussing quite rationally when I should plan to come down. Mary would be on her way tomorrow. Mary's husband Hugh would come the following weekend.

"What I'd really like, John, would be to have you come for my birthday. And meanwhile . . . will you see what you can do about the Egyptians?"

The waiting was hard. I kept hearing from Mary and talked both with her and with Mother regularly on the phone. The operation went well. Within a few days Hugh was able to move Mother into the nursing unit of Westminster Terrace, the very residence Mother was planning to enter when she got old. At first we were encouraged. But as time passed it was apparent that the disorientation which had caused Mother to ask me about "the Egyptians" was continuing. In fact it was happening more frequently.

The night before Mother's birthday, I flew down to Louisville. Scott and Meg, who now lived in Nashville, planned to join me the next morning at Westminster Terrace. It was an eerie experience going into Mother's house, which she and Dad had built twenty years earlier on a corner of the farm where I had spent my vacations as a boy. Dad had not lived to enjoy their dream home. The house was retirement-small, exquisite, every detail done with quality in mind. Through the sliding glass doors out back I could see the small knoll where as a boy I had collected arrowheads simply by walking behind the plow as it bit into the land. Dad had bought Talisman in the Depression; if things got bad enough he could always grow food for the family. Dad died in the same year he and Mother intended to start life in their dream home. Mother made the move anyhow.

Now, little touches spelled out how abruptly she had been forced to leave. There was a cream cheese and olive mixture in the refrigerator. Greenery which she had brought in from the yard was still almost fresh. A copy of the Louisville *Courier Journal* warned drivers to be cautious over the upcoming Memorial Day holidays. This was still a living house. I just did not grasp the fact that Mother herself could really have changed. After all, just a few days ago, she was still running in the academic circles she had known all her life. Mother had taught at Barnard College in New York, she had been Dean of Women at Union Theological, she was still a writer and lecturer—or at least she had been before her fall.

I drove Mother's car (she had just bought a new one) out to Westminster Terrace the next morning. It was as pleasant a place as I remembered it to be. Mother and Tib and I had come here together a year or so ago just to look the place over "for someday." I found her on the second floor of the nursing wing. She was sitting in a wheelchair, a shawl spread across her legs, her head bowed slightly. She looked tired. Gone was the whimsical smile I had seen so often. Mother had thick, naturally wavy hair upswept and framing her face in soft curves. I had never seen a whisp of her hair out of place. Now it was disheveled because as she sat in her chair she kept running the fingers of her left hand, then of her right, upward from temple to crown.

"Mother?"

Mother looked up. Her eyes caught mine and brightened.

"Johnnie!"

She hadn't called me Johnnie for years.

We embraced and then began the strangest of visits. I told Mother that Scott and Meg were coming soon, to help celebrate her birthday. She didn't seem to understand about her birthday, even though the nurses had pasted felt board messages, "Happy Birthday Mrs. Sherrill!" all around the wing.

"It's not my birthday, is it?" Mother asked. She ran her hands up the side of her head. "It couldn't be my birthday because I'm going to Roanoke soon!"

Mother kept drifting in and out of the real world she was living in there on the second floor of Westminster Terrace. She did not like the wheelchair because it had a device in it to keep her from getting up—broken leg or no—and walking out. She kept fumbling with the lock system . . . "Well never mind," she said with an impatient shrug. "Here comes Scott and Meg. We can get out of this thing later."

And for a moment, while we were all greeting each other, Mother was right with us. "Meggie, you're looking so pretty! You've done your hair in a different way!"

"Yes, I got tired of its being long."

A chair scraped across the floor in the hall. Mother cocked her head. "That's the last whistle. I don't want to put pressure on you, but we have to get the bags aboard. Let me ask you . . ." this to a passing nurse . . . "are we on the right platform to Roanoke?"

Scott and Meg turned to me in confusion. "Mother lived in Texas," I explained. "She went to college in Roanoke, Virginia. She was very young. Probably seventeen."

And suddenly, while I was still speaking, I felt the shock of what I had been doing. I was talking *about* Mother in front of her, as though she were not there. Meggie did not make this error. When she had something she wanted to say about Mother, she pulled me aside.

"I wonder," Meg said, "if this 'train trip' doesn't say a lot about how your mother is feeling. She is away from home in a frightening new place. Maybe she's reliving an earlier time when she had to leave her home and go to a new and strange place . . ."

The end of the day saw Mother very tired. Her head began to droop again, and again she started the slow fingering of her hair, first left hand from temple to crown, then the right. A nurse came to get her. A few minutes later the three of us, Scott, Meg and I, were standing beside her bed feeling like the forlorn children we were. Mother complained that they treated her like a baby, strapping her down. "It's just to keep you from getting out of the bed, Mrs. Sherrill," the nurse explained. "We can't have you trying to walk on that leg."

The nurse left. Mother and Scott and Meg and I held hands in a circle around the bed and prayed together. Then we had to go. As we were leaving I turned and had one last glimpse, for now. Mother, lying very flat with her head turned toward me raised her right forearm only—she did not try to lift her whole arm—and waved good-bye.

Scott and Meg returned to Nashville. I went back to New York. Either Mary or I, or Tib or Hugh, or one of our children managed to get to Louisville every few weeks to supplement visits from parts of the family who lived there. Reports continued to be negative: Mother's disorientation grew worse. She had to have a "sitter" (I certainly hope Mother never hears that word!)—first for thirteen hours a day, then eighteen, then around the clock. A wonderful pair of women, Fran Murphy and Jennet Wrighthouse headed the team that spelled each other at the task of trying to keep Mother's mind in the present. On one visit when Tib was with me we tried taking Mother out to lunch. She sat in her wheelchair at the end of the table, hunched over. When she tried to drink her coffee, she had to hold her left hand with her right to still a shaking. With her head leaning forward to sip at the scalding coffee, Mother began to cry, and we realized that we were in one of those worst of all moments —a moment of lucidity. Mother's mind for reasons which the doctors cannot understand snapped in and out of reality. Even as she sat there now she realized where she was, what was happening to her. There was nothing we could do but cry with her.

And so the condition stabilized. The final diagnosis after exhaustive tests was cerebral arteriosclerosis. There was hope that a near miracle drug would help. It did not. Tranquilizers and stimulants were both tried in succession. They did not help either. I finally got around to asking the doctor who headed the team of specialists monitoring Mother's condition what, in his experience, the prognosis was. The doctor was an empathetic man. I could see how much it cost him to use the word because he couched it in a long paragraph that allowed for sudden new discoveries, but nevertheless the doctor finally leaned forward on his desk, supported his chin on a fist he had formed with his left hand and used the word . . . *irreversible*.

I had thought I was beginning to grasp the principle that solving problems isn't as important as staying in the presence of God as we walk through problems. But now, in this circumstance, living this principle proved to be exceedingly difficult. So far, I had been able to say, Yes, I see God as I face the difficulty and I see Him in the solution too. Now suddenly I was faced with a situation where I could not see God in the answer.

I felt frustrated, stymied. Praying in the Spirit was the only kind of prayer-life that seemed to satisfy. Work stagnated. People's well-intentioned offers of help fell on unhearing ears. One emphatic fellow came into my office shouting, "Praise the Lord, John. Everything's going to be all right." He exuded a loud enthusiasm which, I'm afraid came across just as much "in the flesh" as I knew my fatigue and discouragement to be. He called, very loudly, on the Lord then and there to bring complete healing to Mother. He shouted, he claimed, he proclaimed, but my spirit did not tell me that the Holy Spirit was in his positiveness.

The fact of the matter is that we often *are* faced with problems that have no solutions to our liking. People do get desperately sick, loved ones do lose their reason, friends do become so depressed there is no reaching them. Everyone suffers in these situations. Frustration and anger are both present, if we are honest.

It was right at this point that God spoke to me once again, as He so often does, through people.

Gordon and Judy Anderson had been part of our prayer group before they moved south. Gordon was Superintendent of Schools in nearby Yorktown Heights but had accepted an even more challenging position in Frederick, Maryland. Of course, the move meant that the Andersons had to sell their house. That did not seem an insuperable problem. Their home was a roomy colonial, reasonably priced, complete with swimming pool and thousands of hours of prayer in the walls. So they put their house on the market and found a new place in Frederick, located on a maple-lined street within walking distance of Gordon's office. They bought the house and moved in, confident that their Yorktown home would sell in a reasonable time.

But weeks went by. Then months, and the house did not sell.

"Well, the winter season is always slow," we said in our prayer group. "Wait until spring." Spring came: no sale. Summer and fall came: still no sale. All this while the Andersons were carrying two mortgages and a bridge loan. Music lessons and bicycles could wait, mortgage payments couldn't.

One night, after the Andersons' house had been sitting, unsold, for thirteen months, Judy came north for a visit. It was Wednesday night and the prayer group was meeting. Judy hadn't stopped for supper and now she sat on the floor with a malt and a Big Mac in her lap, listening as I recounted the story of Mother. I could almost see her brace herself, as if for an unpleasant task. She put down her malt.

"John, are you fighting?"

Indeed we were. I told Judy how we had taken a stand against the destructive forces that were attacking Mother; I told how we had prayed for her and with her. I filled her in on the medical support measures we were using.

"No that's not what I mean. I want to know if you are fighting to trust the Lord even when you don't *understand* what He's doing?"

Judy shifted her position, took a quick swallow of her malt and went on. She and Gordon had learned about this battle when their house didn't sell. They couldn't *understand* what was happening. "That was the hardest part," she said. "It still is. If we could look into God's heart and see why He wasn't answering the specifics of our prayer it would be so much easier. But He hasn't shown this to us."

"Yet you have managed to stay so confident . . ."

"But not confident that our prayers will be answered to our wishes. Confident instead in our trust. And this is

where the Bible comes in. Because we don't have to *feel*
trusting if we use the Bible correctly. Every day, whether
we feel like it or not we hold onto a Bible promise. That's
how we spend the energy we might have put into worry,
and thrashing around and complaining."

She went on to talk about how she and Gordon affirmed
God's caring in the face of the evidence. I immediately
recognized their selections as Power Verses. "All things
work together for good to them that love God, to them
who are the called according to his purpose" (Romans
8:28 KJV); "My God shall supply all your need according
to his riches in glory by Christ Jesus" (Philippians 4:19
KJV); "Seek ye first the kingdom of God, and his righteousness; and all these things shall be added unto you"
(Matthew 6:33 KJV); "God *is* love" (1 John 4:16 KJV).

"What we are doing," Judy said, summarizing, "is to
let God speak for us when we can't speak for ourselves.
It's not complicated, but it works."

I went home that night realizing that the Andersons had
been given a special ministry while living through their
difficult time. It was the Ministry of Trusting. "A bit ex-
pensive for the Andersons," I said to Tib on the way home,
"but how important for us right now. This is what we
should try every time we don't *understand* what God is
doing. We should trust by letting the Bible speak for us
when we aren't strong enough to speak for ourselves."

The very next week I would be flying down to Kentucky again. I knew what I would find, unless there had
been a change. Mother would be sitting in her wheelchair,
literally tied down. She would look at me from beneath
slightly drooping lids, with those gray-blue eyes of hers,
not understanding. And I would not be able to help except in one way . . . but perhaps it was the most important help of all. I could *trust* for Mother. Even while

she rocked, moving her fingers through her hair, I could quietly trust through His own words: "God is love."

It was while I was getting ready for this trip that I found in the writings of Teilhard de Chardin a different way of stating this trust. Teilhard speaks of Communion through Diminishment:

> When the signs of age begin to mark my body (and still more when they touch my mind); when the ill that is to diminish me or carry me off strikes from without or is born within me; when the painful moment comes in which I suddenly awaken to the fact that I am ill or growing old; and above all at that last moment when I feel I am losing hold of myself and am absolutely passive within the hands of the great unknown forces that have formed me; in all those dark moments, O God, grant that I may understand that it is You (provided only my faith is strong enough) who are painfully parting the fibres of my being in order to penetrate to the very marrow of my substance and bear me away within Yourself.

Teilhard de Chardin
The Divine Milieu

16.

⚬⚬⚬⚬⚬⚬⚬⚬⚬⚬⚬⚬⚬⚬⚬⚬⚬⚬⚬⚬⚬⚬⚬⚬⚬⚬

The Best of All for Last

Feeling things with God:
a new way to read the Bible

I HAVE TO ADMIT that I was dragging my feet on our way to Tarrytown, New York, a twenty-minute drive away from our home. It was a Friday evening, just coming on six o'clock, and I'd much rather be heading out for dinner with Tib than toward a Roman Catholic institution I'd seen for years, but had never visited.

There it was above us now, Marymount, a mammoth red-brick pile covering acres of real estate on a hilltop near the Hudson River. I knew that Marymount had been a fine girls' school, but that like so many once-prospering religious institutions in the Hudson Valley, it had fallen on hard times. A handful of nuns tried to stay together by using the buildings in whatever way came to hand—as a day-care center, as a facility rented out for business conferences and, as in our case, as a meeting place for retreat groups. The weekend to which we were headed was called by the enigmatic and more than a little frightening name, "Marriage Encounter."

Friends had "made a weekend retreat" here. (I noted that Catholics never went on a retreat, they always made

a retreat.) Our friends came back enthusiastic, stating
flatly that Marriage Encounter would change our lives—
which promise was oddly threatening, and perhaps ac-
counted for my present feet-dragging.

But, here we were, turning through the gate into the
grounds of Marymount to be met by a nun in black
habit with glasses as thick as her brogue, who stood in
the driveway directing traffic.

"And a good evening to you. Will you be making the
weekend? Or are you here to help?"

"We're making the weekend," I said through the rolled-
down car window, feeling very Roman.

"Then park, if you would, close by the fence and go
inside."

They put us in a tiny third floor room which overlooked
a stand, down near the driveway, where another smiling
nun was trying to raise a few dollars by selling potted
plants to visitors. I don't know why that glimpse of
dogged bravery put me in a more receptive mind, but it
did: by the time we were seated in a semicircle in the
main conference room downstairs, I was feeling less defensive. There were thirty-one couples in the room, three
of whom had been on this weekend before and were
active as our leaders along with a priest. The priest intrigued me. When his turn came to introduce himself
John Mihelko told us, in a voice so low it was hard to
follow his words, that until his order had been kicked
out he had been a missionary to China. An introspective
man with deepset, shadow-rimmed eyes, John Mihelko
now pastored a church in lower Manhattan's China-
town.

Was everyone else as nervous as I was? The leaders
passed out notebooks and ball-point pens that wrote
sporadically. We sat in silence, wondering what we were
supposed to do.

Two days later, Tib and I stood side by side in our pews in the church-sized chapel of Marymount. Resting on the marble altar at the east end of the sanctuary along with those of the other couples, were the notebooks we had been given last Friday night. We fought back tears of gratitude that we had found each other thirty years before. Gratitude that we had a family that was real, and not just the shell it might have been. Gratitude for the new art we had just learned, symbolized by the notebooks which lay on the altar.

Led by John Mihelko we now repeated our marriage vows. All around us other couples were doing the same. John renewed his priestly vows too. Then, slowly, as couples, we were called forward to the altar to receive from John's hands the two notebooks which we had placed there earlier. John had a personal blessing for each couple. It was a long process, and I found myself reviewing just what these notebooks contained. A special kind of Love Letter, John had called the messages scribbled on their pages. Over this long and exhausting weekend each husband or wife had written to the other many times, letters of a unique quality, meant for his spouse's eyes only. There was no doubt in my mind that in these epistles Marriage Encounter had found a tool Tib and I would always be thankful for.

The concept of Marriage Encounter was born in the early sixties in Spain where a young priest, Gabriel Salvo, was working with couples, trying to help them reaffirm the strength of their marriages. Father Salvo noticed that often, whenever there was unhappiness in the home, the partners had stopped listening to each other's *feelings*. They were dealing exclusively with issues—as important as it was to deal with issues—rather than with each other's emotions. Which was too bad, because it is through feelings that we have the most direct experience of another person. What would happen if these couples could be taught to share their hopes and fears again, just as they had when they first fell in love? As soon as he started to work with this idea Father Salvo discovered a secret. Couples who had been married for a while could communicate better on paper than they could by confronting each other in direct dialogue.

This was the origin of Marriage Encounter. Parents by the thousands came into more creative relationship with each other, children no longer had to act out their anxieties. After a presentation of his findings at Notre Dame in August 1967, an American priest, Father Chuck Gallagher, began to develop the idea here in the United States. Today more than a million men and women have taken part in the Marriage Encounter experience.*

At the heart of Marriage Encounter, then, is the notebook, where each partner writes his Love Letters. We were not to write about issues, but about the emotions which a given issue aroused in us. The key was to avoid judgment, opinion, criticism. Instead we were to center down on one question: "How does that make me feel?"

"Feelings are neither right nor wrong," we were told. "They just are. So write about your emotions without apology." We were assigned starting-point subjects to explore:

What do I like best about you? How does that make me feel?

What do I like best about myself? How does that make me feel?

What do I like best about us? How does that make me feel?

For at least ten minutes we were to write, always ap-

---

* For further information write Marriage Encounter, 567 Morris Avenue, Elizabeth, New Jersey 07208.

plying the yardstick, "Is this a judgment, or am I really sharing the way I feel?"

Then came the second step. When we finished writing, we were to exchange notebooks with each other. We were to absorb the contents of each other's letters. "Read the letter twice," the leaders told us. "Once for what is actually said, and a second time for the person peering, however timidly, through the lines."

After we had written our Love Letter, after we had exchanged and read each other's epistles, we were to talk about the feelings expressed. "For no longer than ten minutes," John Mihelko said. "That's about as long as most people can stick to feelings without getting bogged down in problems and solutions."

So we separated from the group to experiment with our "ten and ten" as Marriage Encounter calls these pairs of write-and-dialogue sessions. We were astonished to discover that there were dozens of feelings we had never explored. Once the first dialogue was completed we returned to the conference room for our next topic, then for another, and another, and another. That first night we dialogued until three in the morning.

We were exhausted, of course. After breakfast the next morning, when we were back in our room ready to face dialogue topic number five, we began to fight. Tib complained that I was not following directions; I complained that she was not listening to what I had to *say*. Then we had an idea. Why not let this very fight be the subject of our next letter to each other?

It turned out, when we joined the semicircle downstairs, that other couples had been fighting too. In fact, we were all going through a marriage in microcosm. After a honeymoon of superb communication came a period of very low communication, bickering and despair. This, the leaders pointed out, was an expected part of every healthy marriage. Other couples had also handled their negative feelings by a "ten and ten," on the spot, and they too not only passed through the disagreement unscathed but had come out on the other side closer than ever to each other.

And now in the chapel at Marymount, John Mihelko was calling our names. Tib and I held hands like a couple of teenagers as we stepped out into the aisle and walked forward to the altar. John's deepset eyes were alive with joy as he placed his hands on our two notebooks and asked the Lord to bless them and urged us to continue our ten-and-ten daily, letting the circumstances of the hour suggest the dialogue.

"You know," John Mihelko said, looking up and speaking to the entire group in that whisper-low voice of his, ". . . you know . . ." he said again, and then John touched on the idea which was to round out my entire adventure with Scripture, ". . . it has always seemed to me that the Bible is God's Love Letter to us. We should read His Letter the way we do our own, twice: once for what is being said and a second time for the Person showing forth between the lines."

The weekend was over. We packed up, putting our notebooks away more carefully than anything else. We went downstairs, bought a couple of house plants from the nun who was at her booth again, went out to our car parked close by the fence. We were fatigued, but we were also certain that we had made a good retreat. Not only because of the new tool we had in our marriage, but because of the whole new way of approaching the Bible that had been suggested at the last moment at the altar.

That same night during my quiet time I found myself looking at the Bible with fresh eyes, thinking about the enormity of the task God has in making Himself known to people. In reaching toward us, perhaps He always takes us through a pattern similar to the one I had experienced. At first, I raced through the Bible, absorbing the joy of shared love. Then, God began to show me that He wanted to be a part of the struggles I was facing: how do you discipline a child, handle an addiction, resolve competitiveness?

Important as these areas were, as revealing as they were of His caring, there was a still more profound way of reading the Bible. I should offer my feelings to Him, and I should try to catch something of *His* feelings too. I should be alert for the Person who was trying, through the medium of human language, somehow to convey the vastness of an unutterable love.

So that night I tried something new to me. I came to the Bible with nothing particular in mind, just letting Him talk to me about our lives together, telling me how He feels about any given situation at hand.

I started to read the Psalm appointed for that evening.

Bless the Lord, O my soul: and all that is within me, bless his holy name. Bless the Lord, O my soul, and forget not all his benefits . . .

Psalm 103:1–2 KJV

Then I imagined what it would be like for God to hear these words being said by His people. "That's good. That's how I want you to feel," He might be saying. "You're beginning to glimpse a fraction of My total, self-giving nature."

I read the entire Psalm with this listening ear, trying to feel things with God. To my mind came other words of His, spoken to Moses on Mt. Sinai. ". . . for I the Lord thy God am a jealous God . . ." (Exodus 20:5 KJV). Jealous, not in a negative, clutching, suspicious way, but jealous as a positive, creative fact. God is jealous because He cares enough for us to want the unique best for us: Himself alone. Our highest goal is to reach toward one prize only, God Himself. We fall short if ever we:

> *use* God . . . I want God at my side so that I can achieve a goal . . .
> *divide* God . . . I love Him and want to serve Him; but to be practical . . .
> *doubt* God . . . I trust God, of course, but . . .

Whenever we do fall for one of these temptations we dilute the richness of the prize, which is closeness to God. God alone is the measure of success in problem-handling. That is where we are headed.

And what is the role of the Bible in pressing toward this mark? I could see it at last. We were at our best when we read the Bible for companionship with God.

God wanted us to use Scripture in the way Jesus did. He wanted us to store up His word, which He would infuse with power in present situations. He wanted us to speak forth His word, sending it into our problems.

But always, He yearned for us to use that Scripture toward the highest goal of all . . . the enjoyment of Himself for Himself alone.

P.S.

Full Circle

I STARTED THIS book commenting that one of the peculiarities of putting something down on paper is that you freeze events at a point in time.

This has happened again. I have described what occurred in my mother's life when she fell, then proceeded to slip into a greater and greater disorientation. Three weeks ago, when I had finished this book and was at the point of sending it to the printer, we had a telephone call from one of Mother's companions with the surprising news that Mother had been asking what year it was. Later we had a call from Margaret Durham: she had just been to see Mother, " . . . and John, she knew who she was. And who I was. And that we were at Westminster Terrace."

Two days later still, a *letter* arrived. The handwriting was perhaps a bit shaky, but unmistakably Mother's. I called a staff member at the nursing home. Yes, Mother seemed to be somewhat improved, but we weren't to expect too much.

"We had a letter from her today," I said.

Yes, some of the sitters were thoughtful that way. They wrote letters for our residents.

"No, this was from Mother herself."

Silence. "Are you sure you know her handwriting?"

What an interesting question. "I'm sure."

"Well . . . let me . . . I'll call you back."

The same note of bewilderment came from all the other professionals I talked with on the phone. The diagnosis had been cerebral arteriosclerosis but now it was clear that this could not have been correct. We were all in a quandary. We could neither tell what had gone wrong in the first place, nor what had gone right in the second place. No matter, the outlook was still most positive.

During those long telephone discussions I kept remembering what we had learned when the news from Mother was *not* good. A visible and happy outcome to our problems was not the yardstick that told us whether or not Mother was safe in God's hands. The yardstick was what we knew about God. He tells us in a thousand ways that once He has chosen us He will—incredibly—make all things come out right. So, although Mother's news was unbelievably good today, we had in fact already received the best news of all for her that, whether things seem right or not, whether we understand what He is doing or not, we could always be confident that He was doing better things for her than we could dream of.

Tib and I flew to Kentucky to see The Walking Wonder, as Mother proudly said people were calling her. The thing I remember most about the visit is that Mother was Mother again. As simple as that. The light was back in her eyes.

One thing bothered her more than all else. She remembered nothing about the eleven past months, none of our visits, none of the medical consultations, none of her train trips to Roanoke. So she spent a lot of time trying to fill herself in on her "missing eleven."

But she was not resisting the fact that her old lifestyle had changed. There was a family celebration dinner at the Owl Creek Country Club, opposite Mother's just-sold house. Mother wanted to see her home before dinner. So we drove into the crunchy gravel driveway, somewhat overrun by grass now since there was no one in the house yet. Mother had only one comment. "I hope the new people will be as happy there as I was."

At dinner, surrounded by family, Mother had everyone laughing. It was a good, good evening. Mother proudly announced that tomorrow she was moving into a room all her own, downstairs, away from the greater-care unit. She'd have a phone and a good light to read by and just outside her window she planned to put in a few bulbs for next spring, which is a year away.

We took Mother back so late that we had to ring the night bell to get in, but she seemed only normally tired. The last I saw of her that evening, she was walking unaided across her room to get something from her bureau.

Suddenly Mother caught sight of herself in the mirror. Up went her hand, starting the familiar gesture I had watched so often here before, when Mother used to sit in her wheelchair running her fingers restlessly up the side of her head, temple to crown.

But something must have told her now that this was a gesture of hopelessness which belonged to the past. For at the last moment instead of completing the movement, Mother shifted her hand and patted into place a stray lock of hair.

Appendix One

My Arsenal

These are the 100 Bible passages which I memorized. Each individual's arsenal of Scripture will be different, of course, fitted to his own warfare.

My particular choices do not even attempt to provide a balanced survey of Biblical resources; on the contrary, each one was chosen to meet a specific need and reflects my rather one-track preoccupation at the time.

Unless otherwise noted, all quotations are from the King James Version.

The goal of Bible reading:

1. Mine eyes are ever toward the Lord; for he shall pluck my feet out of the net. (Psalm 25:15)

Jesus' Master Plan
for Handling Problems:

2. THE FIRST TEMPTATION. And Jesus being full of the Holy Ghost returned from Jordan, and was led by the Spirit into the wilderness, being forty days tempted of the devil. And in those days he did eat nothing: and when they were ended, he afterward hungered. And the devil said unto him, If thou be the Son of God, command this stone that it be made bread. And Jesus answered him,

saying, It is written, That man shall not live by bread alone, but by every word of God. (Luke 4:1–4)

3. THE SECOND TEMPTATION. And the devil, taking him up into an high mountain, showed unto him all the kingdoms of the world in a moment of time. And the devil said unto him, All this power will I give thee, and the glory of them: for that is delivered unto me; and to whomsoever I will I give it. If thou therefore wilt worship me, all shall be thine. And Jesus answered and said unto him, Get thee behind me, Satan: for it is written, Thou shalt worship the Lord thy God, and him only shalt thou serve. (Luke 4:5–8)

4. THE THIRD TEMPTATION. And he brought him to Jerusalem, and set him on a pinnacle of the temple, and said unto him, If thou be the Son of God, cast thyself down from hence: For it is written, He shall give his angels charge over thee, to keep thee: And in their hands they shall bear thee up, lest at any time thou dash thy foot against a stone. And Jesus answering said unto him, It is said, Thou shalt not tempt the Lord thy God.

And when the devil had ended all the temptation, he departed from him for a season. And Jesus returned in the power of the Spirit into Galilee: (Luke 4:9–14a)

Do I dare talk about
my own temptations?

5. For there is nothing hid, which shall not be manifested; neither was anything kept secret, but that it should come abroad. (Mark 4:22)

6. Thou hast set our iniquities before thee, our secret sins in the light of thy countenance. (Psalm 90:8)

Where temptations come from:

7. Put on the whole armour of God, that ye may be able to stand against the wiles of the devil. For we wrestle not against flesh and blood, but against principalities, against powers, against the rulers of the darkness of this world, against spiritual wickedness in high places. (Ephesians 6:11, 12)

Where strength to resist comes from:

8. God hath spoken once; twice have I heard this; that power belongeth unto God. (Psalm 62:11)

9. Pull me out of the net that they have laid privily for me: for thou art my strength. (Psalm 31:4)

10. Stand therefore, having your loins girt about with truth, and having on the breastplate of righteousness; and your feet shod with the preparation of the gospel of peace; above all, taking the shield of faith, wherewith ye shall be able to quench all the fiery darts of the wicked. And take the helmet of salvation, and the sword of the Spirit, which is the word of God: (Ephesians 6:14–17)

11. Give unto the Lord, O ye mighty, give unto the Lord glory and strength. (Psalm 29:1)

12. Finally, my brethren, be strong in the Lord, and in the power of his might. (Ephesians 6:10)

Before reading the newspaper:

13. I would have you wise unto that which is good, and simple concerning evil. (Romans 16:19b)

When I'm under time pressure:

14. My times are in thy hand: deliver me from the hand of mine enemies, and from them that persecute me. (Psalm 31:15)

An image that helps me picture
the focused power of God:

15. But if I with the finger of God cast out devils, no doubt the kingdom of God is come upon you. (Luke 11:20)

Against negative thought patterns:

16. Be ye transformed by the renewing of your mind. (Romans 12:2a)

17. Therefore, putting aside all filthiness and all that remains of wickedness, in humility receive the word implanted, which is able to save your souls. (James 1:21 NAS)

18. Finally, brethren, whatsoever things are true, whatsoever things are honest, whatsoever things are just, whatsoever things are pure, whatsoever things are lovely, whatsoever things are of good report; if there be any virtue, and if there be any praise, think on these things. (Philippians 4:8)

When my God get too small:

19. How oft did they provoke him in the wilderness, and grieve him in the desert! Yea, they turned back and tempted God, and limited the Holy One of Israel. (Psalm 78:40, 41)

When I have to take a trip:

20. For though I be absent in the flesh, yet am I with you in the spirit, joying and beholding your order, and the stedfastness of your faith in Christ. (Colossians 2:5)

I'm apprehensive:

21. Fear thou not; for I am with thee: be not dismayed; for I am thy God: I will strengthen thee; yea, I will help thee; yea, I will uphold thee with the right hand of my righteousness. (Isaiah 41:10)

My work was planned ahead of time:

22. For we are his workmanship, created in Christ Jesus unto good works, which God hath before ordained that we should walk in them. (Ephesians 2:10)

Controlling Physical Appetites:

23. Dearly beloved, I beseech you as strangers and pilgrims, abstain from fleshy lusts, which war against the soul. (1 Peter 2:11)

*When I don't seem
to be getting anywhere:*

24. And it came to pass, when Pharaoh had let the people go, that God led them not through the way of the land of the Philistines, although that was near; for God said, Lest peradventure the people repent when they see war, and they return to Egypt: But God led the people about, through the way of the wilderness of the Red sea: . . . (Exodus 13:17, 18a)

A mealtime grace:

25. The eyes of all wait upon thee; and thou givest them their meat in due season. Thou openest thine hand, and satisfiest the desire of every living thing. (Psalm 145:15, 16)

Grace when dieting:

26. [The Lord] satisfieth thy mouth with good things; so that thy youth is renewed like the eagle's. (Psalm 103:5)

Lines from His Love Letter:

27. The friendship of the Lord is for those who fear him, and he makes known to them his covenant. (Psalm 25:14 RSV)

28. . . . he will joy over thee with singing. (Zephaniah 3:17)

29. [The Lord . . .] grant thee according to thine own heart, and fulfill all thy counsel. (Psalm 20:4)

30. Take delight in the Lord, and he will give you the desires of your heart. (Psalm 37:4 RSV)

My reply:

31. Bless the Lord, O my soul: and all that is in within me, bless his holy name. (Psalm 103:1)

32. Because thy lovingkindness is better than life, my lips shall praise thee. (Psalm 63:3)

*Len LeSourd's key verse
for Chosen Books:*

33. Commit your way to the Lord; trust in him, and he will act. (Psalm 37:5 RSV)

I must make a decision:

34. What man is he that feareth the Lord? him shall he teach in the way that he shall choose. (Psalm 25:12)

35. . . . for thy name's sake lead me, and guide me. (Psalm 31:3)

Before temptation arises:

36. . . . choose you this day whom ye will serve . . . as for me and my house, we will serve the Lord. (Joshua 24:15)

When it does: God is in this too:

37. For thou, O God, hast tested us; thou hast tried us as silver is tried. (Psalm 66:10 RSV)

*Openness to God and
to my neighbor:*

38. Take heed what ye hear: with what measure ye mete, it shall be measured to you: and unto you that hear shall more be given. For he that hath, to him shall be given:

and he that hath not, from him shall be taken even that which he hath. (Mark 4:24, 25)

Everything speaks of Him:

39. Let the floods clap their hands: let the hills be joyful together before the Lord . . . (Psalm 98:8, 9a)

On opening the Bible:

40. For the word of God is quick, and powerful, and sharper than any twoedged sword, piercing even to the dividing asunder of soul and spirit, and of the joints and marrow, and is a discerner of the thoughts and intents of the heart. (Hebrews 4:12)

On closing the Bible:

41. I rejoice at thy word, as one that findeth great spoil. (Psalm 119:162)

When I'm tired:

42. In returning and rest shall ye be saved; in quietness and in confidence shall be your strength. (Isaiah 30:15a)

43. He giveth power to the faint; and to them that have no might he increaseth strength. (Isaiah 40:29)

44. And let us not be weary in well doing: for in due season we shall reap, if we faint not. (Galatians 6:9)

For a dry spell:

45. O God, thou art my God; early will I seek thee: my soul thirsteth for thee, my flesh longeth for thee in a dry and thirsty land, where no water is; to see thy power and thy glory, so as I have seen thee in the sanctuary. (Psalm 63:1, 2)

When I am wrongly criticized:

46. Princes have persecuted me without a cause: but my heart standeth in awe of thy word. (Psalm 119:161)

47. For what glory is it, if, when ye be buffeted for your faults, ye shall take it patiently? but if, when ye do well, and suffer for it, ye take it patiently, this is acceptable with God. (1 Peter 2:20)

48. [Speaking of Jesus:] Who, when he was reviled, reviled not again; when he suffered, he threatened not; but com-

mitted himself to him that judgeth righteously. (1 Peter 2:23)

49. The Lord executeth righteousness and judgment for all that are oppressed. (Psalm 103:6)

50. From thee let my vindication come! Let thy eyes see the right. (Psalm 17:2 rsv)

When I am rightly criticized:

51. Bless the Lord, O my soul, and forget not all his benefits: who forgiveth all thine iniquities; who healeth all thy diseases; who redeemeth thy life from destruction; who crowneth thee with lovingkindness and tender mercies. (Psalm 103:2–4)

52. The Lord is merciful and gracious, slow to anger, and plenteous in mercy. (Psalm 103:8)

53. He will not always chide: neither will he keep his anger forever. (Psalm 103:9)

54. He hath not dealt with us after our sins; nor rewarded us according to our iniquities. For as the heaven is high above the earth, so great is his mercy toward them that fear him. As far as the east is from the west, so far hath he removed our transgressions from us. (Psalm 103:10–12)

55. Like as a father pitieth his children, so the Lord pitieth them that fear him. For he knoweth our frame; he remembereth that we are dust. (Psalm 103:13, 14)

Singlemindedness in the
midst of multiplicity:

56. . . . this one thing I do, forgetting those things which are behind, and reaching forth unto those things which are before, I press toward the mark for the prize of the high calling of God in Christ Jesus. (Philippians 3:13, 14)

The 55-mile speed limit:

57. Submit yourselves therefore to every ordinance of man for the Lord's sake. (1 Peter 2:13a)

My writing "commission":

58. Write the things which thou hast seen, and the things which are, and the things which shall be hereafter . . . (Revelation 1:19)

When I face something I'm afraid of:

59. For we have not an high priest which cannot be touched with the feeling of our infirmities; but was in all points tempted like as we are, yet without sin. Let us therefore come boldly unto the throne of grace, that we may obtain mercy, and find grace to help in time of need. (Hebrews 4:15, 16)

60. For you did not receive the spirit of slavery to fall back into fear, but you have received the spirit of sonship. (Romans 8:15 RSV)

Moment-by-moment inspiration:

61. But when they shall lead you, and deliver you up, take no thought beforehand what ye shall speak, neither do you premeditate: but whatsoever shall be given you in that hour, that speak ye: for it is not ye that speak, but the Holy Ghost. (Mark 13:11)

Getting my priorities straight:

62. So teach us to number our days, that we may apply our hearts unto wisdom. (Psalm 90:12)

63. As for man, his days are as grass: as a flower of the field, so he flourisheth. For the wind passeth over it, and it is gone; and the place thereof shall know it no more. (Psalm 103:15, 16)

Loving my fellow Christians:

64. Then Peter opened his mouth, and said, Of a truth I perceive that God is no respecter of persons: But in every nation he that feareth him, and worketh righteousness, is accepted with him. (Acts 10:34, 35)

65. As for the saints in the land, they are the noble, in whom is all my delight. (Psalm 16:3 RSV)

When my heart can't contain
my love for Him:

66. Bless the Lord, ye his angels, that excel in strength, that do his commandments, hearkening unto the voice of his

word. Bless ye the Lord, all ye his hosts; ye ministers of his, that do his pleasure. Bless the Lord, all his works in all places of his dominion: bless the Lord, O my soul. (Psalm 103:20–22)

When I'm depressed:

67. Why art thou cast down, O my soul? and why art thou disquieted within me? hope thou in God: for I shall yet praise him who is the health of my countenance, and my God. (Psalm 42:11)

When things seem to go wrong:

68. The Lord hath prepared his throne in the heavens; and his kingdom ruleth over all. (Psalm 103:19)

Illness, for instance:

69. And he said unto me, My grace is sufficient for thee: for my strength is made perfect in weakness. Most gladly therefore will I rather glory in my infirmities, that the power of Christ may rest upon me. (2 Corinthians 12:9)

And evil. God is in ultimate control even of this:

70. But as for you, ye thought evil against me; but God meant it unto good, to bring to pass, as it is this day, to save much people alive. (Genesis 50:20)

71. I know that thou canst do all things, and that no purpose of thine can be thwarted. (Job 42:2 RSV)

When I must handle the business side of Chosen Books:

72. Lay not up for yourselves treasures upon earth, where moth and rust doth corrupt, and where thieves break through and steal: But lay up for yourselves treasures in heaven, where neither moth nor rust doth corrupt,

and where thieves do not break through nor steal: For
where your treasure is, there will your heart be also.
(Matthew 6:19–21)

73. If riches increase, set not your heart upon them. (Psalm
62:10)

Once God has given me the victory:

74. For if we sin wilfully after that we have received the
knowledge of the truth, there remaineth no more sacrifice for sins, but a certain fearful looking for of judgment and fiery indignation. (Hebrews 10:26, 27a)

75. For all this they sinned still, and believed not for his
wondrous works. Therefore their days did he consume
in vanity, and their years in trouble. (Psalm 78:32, 33)

76. It is a fearful thing to fall into the hands of the living
God. (Hebrews 10:31)

*A verse Tib gave me
when I wasn't sure I had the victory:*

77. And the Lord said unto Moses in Midian, Go, return
into Egypt: for all the men are dead which sought thy
life. (Exodus 4:19)

Sticking with it:

78. . . . praying always with all prayer and supplication in
the Spirit, and watching thereunto with all persever-
ance and supplication for all saints. (Ephesians 6:18)

79. I made haste, and delayed not to keep thy commandments. (Psalm 119:60)

Promises, when I stick with it:

80. But the mercy of the Lord is from everlasting to everlasting upon them that fear him, and his righteousness
unto children's children; to such as keep his covenant,
and to those that remember his commandments to do
them. (Psalm 103:17, 18)

81. And he shall be like a tree planted by the rivers of
water, that bringeth forth his fruit in his season; his
leaf also shall not wither; and whatsoever he doeth shall
prosper. (Psalm 1:3)

82. (You have . . .) an inheritance incorruptible, and undefiled, and that fadeth not away, reserved in heaven for you. (1 Peter 1:4)

83. For to be carnally minded is death; but to be spiritually minded is life and peace. (Romans 8:6)

When I begin to think this uphill
Christian walk was my own idea:

84. . . . according as he hath chosen us in him before the foundation of the world . . . (Ephesians 1:4)

One reason for suffering:

85. Who comforteth us in all our tribulation, that we may be able to comfort them which are in any trouble, by the comfort wherewith we ourselves are comforted of God (2 Corinthians 1:4)

Another reason:

86. Now no chastening for the present seemeth to be joyous, but grievous: nevertheless afterward it yieldeth the peaceable fruit of righteousness unto them which are exercised thereby. (Hebrews 12:11)

87. The fear of the Lord is the beginning of knowledge: but fools despise wisdom and instruction. (Proverbs 1:7)

88. For I reckon that the sufferings of this present time are not worthy to be compared with the glory which shall be revealed in us. (Romans 8:18)

When I don't know how to pray:

89. Likewise the Spirit also helpeth our infirmities: for we know not what we should pray for as we ought: but the Spirit itself maketh intercession for us with groanings which cannot be uttered. (Romans 8:26)

90. And he that searcheth the hearts knoweth what is the mind of the Spirit, because he maketh intercession for the saints according to the will of God. (Romans 8:27)

Chuck Colson's verse for opening
every Chosen Books board meeting:

91. But we will give ourselves continually to prayer, and to the ministry of the word. (Acts 6:4)

When we can't see where we're going:

92. By faith Abraham, when he was called to go out into a place which he should after receive for an inheritance, obeyed; and he went out, not knowing whither he went. (Hebrews 11:8)

When I'm immobilized by worry:

93. Be careful for nothing; but in every thing by prayer and supplication with thanksgiving let your requests be made known unto God. And the peace of God, which passeth all understanding, shall keep your hearts and minds through Christ Jesus. (Philippians 4:6, 7)

Or by guilt:

94. Jesus . . . saith unto them, They that are whole have no need of the physician, but they that are sick: I came not to call the righteous, but sinners to repentance. (Mark 2:17)

95. There is therefore now no condemnation to them which are in Christ Jesus, who walk not after the flesh, but after the Spirit. (Romans 8:1)

My alcohol Power Verse:

96. Submit yourselves therefore to God. Resist the devil, and he will flee from you. (James 4:7)

My Power Verse for work:

97. And lead us not into temptation, but deliver us from evil: For thine is the kingdom, and the power, and the glory, for ever. Amen. (Matthew 6:13)

The Bible as guide:

98. Thy word is a lamp unto my feet, and a light unto my path. (Psalm 119:105)

The Bible as protection:

99. Order my steps in thy word: and let not any iniquity have dominion over me. (Psalm 119:133)

100. Thy word have I hid in mine heart, that I might not sin against thee. (Psalm 119:11)

The Bible as the way to:

101. Seek the Lord, and his strength: seek his face evermore. (Psalm 105:4)

Appendix Two

Bible Reading Programs

1. Lectionaries:	a) Episcopalian	—*The Church Lesson Calendar* Morehouse-Barlow Co. 78 Danbury Road Wilton, Conn. 06897
	b) Lutheran	—*The New Lectionary* Fortress Press 2900 Queen Lane Philadelphia, Pa. 19129
	c) Presbyterian	—*The Worship Book* The Westminster Press 902 Witherspoon Bldg. Philadelphia, Pa. 19107
	d) Roman Catholic	—*The Ordo* The Paulist Press 545 Island Road Rumsey, N.J. 07446

2. *The Moravian Daily Texts*
The Moravian Board of Education
5 Market Street
Bethlehem, Pa. 18018

Peter Marshall's favorite. One of the first daily devotional books. Came out originally in 1731, and has been published continuously ever since.

3. Scripture Union
1716 Spruce St.
Philadelphia, Pa.
19103

a) *Daily Bread* —An in-depth Bible study.
Goes through the Bible
in four years. Interpretive
comment on Scripture
passages as an aid for
daily Bible reading and
and prayer.

b) *Discovery* —Moves consecutively
through Bible, covering
10–15 verses a day.
Takes reader through the
New Testament twice
and most of Old
Testament once every
four years.

c) *Bible Study Book* —Designed to cover the
whole Bible along with
Commentary. Program
completed in five years.

d) *Bible Characters
and Doctrines* —Sections presenting both
characters and doctrines
in each book providing
balance and variety in the
selected subjects. Four
years to complete.

4. *Daily Light*
Samuel Bagster
and Sons Ltd.
72 Marylebone
Lane
London Wl,
England

A selection of verses for every morning and evening.
A classic devotional text using words of Scripture.

5. *Search the
Scriptures*
Inter-Varsity Press
Downers Grove,
Ill. 60515

Three year program of study, provides variety.
Similar to Inter-Varsity's *Search the Scriptures* is
John Baillie's *Diary of Private Reading*, Charles
Scribner's Sons, N.Y., N.Y.

6. *My Utmost for
His Highest*
by Oswald
Chambers
Dodd, Mead
& Company
79 Madison Ave.
N.Y., N.Y.

Selections for every day of the year—for the Christian
who is eager to be challenged by unusual insights.

7. *Daily Walk* A Scripture reading and comment on given
   The Navigators passages. Covers entire Bible.
   P. O. Box 20
   Colorado Springs,
     Colo. 80901